"A must-have on every leader's bookshelf! BH Tan weaves together the key essentials of global leadership today. In the digital age, leaders are most effective when they embrace a paradoxical mindset. This lies at the intersection of Eastern and Western thinking."

— **Trishia S. Lichauco, PCC**
Leadership Development Coach

"A book whose time has come. Through 25 critical perspectives, it powerfully awakens in us an opportunity to examine the way we habitually think, decide and act. In the digital age, leaders can impact and transform the world through adopting and applying a wholistic East-West resonance code."

— **Marjorie J. Woo, PhD, MCC**
Director, ICF Professional Coaches Global Board

"By far one of the most compelling books on leadership written. Modern leadership styles will be more effective by integrating Asian wisdom with Western thinking. The chapter Humble Leadership exemplifies leadership that people, teams and corporations will rally behind."

— **Don Huang**
Business Development Director (China),
L'Oreal Travel Retail

"BH Tan never fails to impress with his ability to highlight simple values that we tend to forget in our hectic working lives. 'Trust', 'Humble' and 'Listen' are core when we are leading high-performing teams regardless of which side of the world we are working in."

— **Aida Mohamed**
Human Resources Director, Malaysia & Brunei
Zuellig Pharma Sdn Bhd

The WAY of the
LEADER

25 IDEAS FOR LEADING WISELY
IN THE DIGITAL AGE

BH Tan

Marshall Cavendish
Business

© 2021 BH Tan

Reprinted 2020

Published in 2021 by Marshall Cavendish Business
An imprint of Marshall Cavendish International

A member of the
Times Publishing Group

Other Marshall Cavendish Offices:
Marshall Cavendish Corporation, 800 Westchester Ave, Suite N-641, Rye Brook,
NY 10573, USA • Marshall Cavendish International (Thailand) Co Ltd, 253 Asoke,
16th Floor, Sukhumvit 21 Road, Klongtoey Nua, Wattana, Bangkok 10110, Thailand
• Marshall Cavendish (Malaysia) Sdn Bhd, Times Subang, Lot 46, Subang Hi-Tech
Industrial Park, Batu Tiga, 40000 Shah Alam, Selangor Darul Ehsan, Malaysia

Marshall Cavendish is a registered trademark of Times Publishing Limited

National Library Board, Singapore Cataloguing-in-Publication Data
Name(s): Tan, B. H. (Boon Hock), 1953-
Title: The way of the leader : 25 ideas for leading wisely in the digital age / BH Tan.
Description: Singapore : Marshall Cavendish Business, 2021. | Includes index.
Identifier(s): OCN 1245250041 | ISBN 978-981-4928-87-8
Subject(s): LCSH: Leadership. | Management.
Classification: DDC 658.409--dc23

Printed in Singapore

To my granddaughters, Charlotte and Eleanor,
future women leaders

CONTENTS

INTRODUCTION

Asia is on the rise in the global economy. After centuries of Western economic dominance, China, India, and the rest of the East, alongside emerging economies, are beginning to challenge the West for positions of global industry leadership. According to the UK-based Centre for Economics and Business Research (CEBR), China will leapfrog the US to become the world's largest economy by 2028, five years earlier than the previous forecast due to the contrasting recovery of the two countries from the Covid-19 pandemic. Meanwhile, India is tipped to become the third-largest economy by 2030.

A question that begs an answer is, "Henceforth, how will the underlying managerial philosophies and traditions of the various cultures in Asia be positioned on the world stage?"

This is an important topic to address. For many decades now, the West has been the unchallenged leader in thinking about business and leadership. As the pace of globalization quickened, Western multinationals set up subsidiaries around the world. Along with transferring their technologies, bringing jobs to millions, they also exported their managerial philosophy and processes. These Western ideas have been adopted with enthusiasm and applied diligently in both emerging and developed markets worldwide.

In the 1980s and 1990s, the Japanese success in manufacturing won the admiration of the West. This led to a global adoption of Japanese concepts such as quality control circles, teamwork and JIT (Just-In-Time) manufacturing.

Will the rise of China and India bring an infusion of Eastern perspectives to the field of leadership?

All ideas are good, especially if they are diverse. In the history of human experience, the most fruitful developments take place at the intersection of different lines of thought. We can't get anything in starker contrast than the ideas and traditions of the East and West.

The world has entered the digital economy. In 2016, Klaus Schwab, founder and executive chairman of the Geneva-based World Economic Forum (WEF), coined the term the Fourth Industrial Revolution or Industry 4.0. Schwab argued a technological revolution is underway "that is blurring the lines between the physical, digital and biological spheres." Increasingly AI (Artificial Intelligence) will supplant many aspects of the "hard" elements of leadership – those responsible for the raw cognitive processing of facts. This will lead to a greater emphasis on the "soft" aspects of leadership – the behaviors, relationships and attitudes that encourage and motivate people to bring the best versions of themselves to work.

How then should leadership be defined? A recent study by the MIT Sloan School of Management concluded that organizations can no longer lead the way they have been used to in the past. Top-down, bureaucratic, bottomline-driven hierarchies have no place in the new era. More lateral, collaborative, purpose-driven teamwork will be the norm. Leaders will act as facilitators and coaches, and must be ready to empower their teams to come up with solutions on their own. Being able to build trust will be a key attribute, and they must have a healthy dose of humility. Having a passion for technology will be a must.

In the last few decades, there has been a lot of research that points to different thinking styles between Westerners (primarily Europeans, Americans, and citizens of the British Commonwealth) and East Asians (principally the people of China, Korea and Japan). This is reported by psychologist Richard Nisbett in his seminal book entitled *The Geography of Thoughts: How Asians and Westerners Think Differently... and Why.* Kaiping Peng, Nisbett's colleague from China, summarizes the differences very precisely: "You know, the difference between you and me is that I think the world is a circle, and you think it's a line."

Western linearity is displayed in the general belief that the universe is divided into two opposites with a clear-cut demarcation between them: man and nature, subject and object, mind and matter, the divine and the secular. Though the coexistence of opposites is recognized, they are viewed as separate and opposing, resulting in an either-or orientation. Linear thinking proceeds by breaking the world into manageable chunks and tackling them in isolation from each other.

From this mechanistic and fragmented worldview, problems are solved through an analytical, rational and logical process, proceeding in a straight line, making connections in a sequential order. Westerners have a compelling need to find out who is right in an argument. Their form of argumentation is to proceed from thesis to antithesis, and on to synthesis. It focuses the mind wonderfully but may cause tension as the reason for a critique may not be to understand another's viewpoint but to disprove it.

The either-or mindset leads to dualistic thinking. It assumes a universe where there are only two contrasting, mutually exclusive choices or realities: right versus wrong, white versus black, good versus bad, winners versus losers. This becomes a zero-sum game. Nonetheless, this relentless search for the truth underpins the West's undisputed superiority in scientific discoveries. Westerners possess a remarkable sense of personal agency that they are in charge of their own lives and are free to act as they choose. In a word, they believe in individualism.

Chinese circularity takes a more organic and ecological worldview. It sees all things in the universe as constantly changing in a cyclical motion. Nature (and hence organizations) is a self-organizing system in perpetual interaction of *yin* and *yang* forces or energies. Asians attend to objects in their broader context. The world seems more complex to Asians than to Westerners. And understanding events always requires consideration of a host of factors that may interact with each other in unpredictable ways. Formal linear logic plays a lesser role in problem-solving in the complex world that we live in. Chinese culture views opposites as complementary and interdependent. Instead of treating them separately, they are juxtaposed side by side in order to better understand the overall picture. Hence the treatment of opposites is to embrace them in a both-and orientation.

At the interpersonal and organizational levels, this approach has immense benefits as the Chinese's view of life is that it is full of contradictions and that both sides have flaws and virtues. The preferred way of resolving differences is through consensus rather than conflict as only through consensus can sustainable solutions be attained. Another upside is that East Asians may be better able to embrace paradoxes and derive creative solutions.

But the tendency to find the middle way has hampered their efforts to seek out scientific truth through aggressive argumentation. The Chinese counterpart to personal agency and individualism is harmony and collectivism.

"Reality is a circle and we think in a straight line... And we wonder why our deepest problems remain unsolved."
Peter Senge, MIT Sloan School of Management

The title of this book is borrowed from the *Dao De Jing* (or *Tao Te Ching*), the classic Chinese manual on the art of living, governance and leadership written around 500 BCE. *Dao De Jing*, or simply The Dao, can be translated as The Book of the Way. Of its real authorship, there is some uncertainty, but it is generally attributed to Laozi (or Lao Tzu), an older contemporary of Confucius. His name means Old Master, or more picturesquely, Old Boy. Little is known about Laozi except that he could have been an archive-keeper during the Warring States period in ancient China.

The Dao was drawn from Laozi's close observations of nature. It reveals the wisdom of living systems, describing the patterns of energy within and around us. The Chinese call this vital energy *qi*, and the

Japanese call it *ki*. The Dao consists of 81 poems, written with grace and large-heartedness. They radiate a sense of warm humor and deep wisdom. It is the most translated book in history together with the Bible and the Quran. The Dao's influence on the thinking of East Asians is subtle, pervasive and sublime. To understand the thinking habits of East Asians, becoming familiar with the Dao is the first step.

In the course of my leadership consulting work, I have worked with organizations on numerous leadership challenges. Many of these are timeless themes, and I have curated 25 topics that form the basis of this book. As we enter the age of digital transformation, leaders will no doubt be grappling with them again and again. Through real-life cases, you will be exposed to the thinking, decisions and actions of the various protagonists. They are a mix of historical figures, eminent business and political leaders, and ordinary people placed in tough situations, Easterners and Westerners alike. What would you do if you were in their shoes?

My invitation to the reader is to treat each topic as an opportunity to examine how you habitually think, decide and act. There is no right or wrong answer. Your perspective depends on a number of underlying factors such as your experience, culture and worldview. The contrast between your worldview and other mental models may hopefully stimulate novel ideas in making sense of our rapidly changing and unpredictable environment.

As we go through the various topics in this book, some verses from the Dao will be shared. Laozi's teachings are deeply rooted in his love for nature, people and society. The most fundamental of his teachings is that human beings are part of nature. For people to lead rewarding and meaningful lives, they need to conduct their affairs in harmony with – and not in opposition to – nature. Instead of ceaseless striving, becoming more self-aware and doing a little less in a measured way may be a better option.

Looking at the devastation of the ecosystem, untold human sufferings and endless war and conflicts unleashed on the world, we realize that Laozi is right. We have become too sure of our science and technology, and convinced that man is the master of nature. At first blush, Laozi's ideas may sound counter-intuitive. With patience, reflection and curiosity, we gradually become aware of their wisdom.

"When the student is ready, the teacher appears."
Buddhist adage

This book is an exploration of ideas and alternative ways of making sense of situations. We all are used to the linear way of thinking. That's what we've been taught in schools. Now let's find out more about the circular way of thinking. The linearity-versus-circularity difference in Western and Chinese cultures is merely a matter of degree. There is no absolute distinction between the two cultures. Exceptions are numerous and counter-evidence exists. To compare them is not to judge which is superior, but to promote mutual understanding.

Albert Einstein was once asked, "Dr. Einstein, why is it when the mind of man has stretched so far as to discover the structure of the atom we have been unable to devise the political means to the keep the atom from destroying us?" The great scientist replied, "This is simple, my friend. It is because politics is more difficult than physics."

In the view of Professor Peng, now at Tsinghua University, the peoples of the East and the West can learn from each other in fundamental ways. The Chinese can learn much from Western methods of determining scientific truth. And Americans could profit enormously from the Chinese tolerance for accepting contradictions in social, business and political life.

In this very complex, chaotic yet interconnected world that we live in, being able to integrate both streams of thinking can only help us to lead more wisely and courageously. Our time horizon must extend beyond the here and now. The well-being of the generations to come depends on how the present generation thinks and acts.

1

LEADERSHIP PARADOXES

**Treating opposites as complementary leads
to a wealth of creative solutions**

*"Being and non-being create each other.
Difficult and easy support each other.
Long and short define each other.
High and low depend on each other.
Before and after follow each other."*
Laozi

In organizations, we are constantly faced with conflicting demands. They pose dilemmas and result in tensions. Many of them defy common sense and logic, and are difficult to understand. As the business environment gets more complex, they may even seem impossible to address. Here are some examples of conflicting demands:

- Results-orientation and people-focused
- Taking cost out while improving quality
- Short-term and long-term focus
- Digitization with the human touch
- Implementing a major strategic shift without destabilizing the company

When leaders are faced with these paradoxes, the opposing goals cause tension and polarization in the organization. They feel the pressure to make decisions quickly and keep a steady course. But prioritizing one goal will not make the other goal disappear. While it gives a false sense of decisiveness, critical thinking becomes the first casualty. This may trigger a whole host of ramifications, creating even bigger problems for these leaders and their companies. How then can they avoid falling into this trap?

We'll now look at the nature of paradoxes and examine a case study of how one well-known company creatively manages them. Finally, we'll discuss a process for navigating organizational paradoxes.

Understanding paradoxes

For a long time, the Western view of the world has been that of a machine. Whenever a problem is encountered, all that's needed to solve it is first to reduce it to the smallest components for analysis. Next, use a linear cause-and-effect relationship to establish the cause of the problem. Addressing this cause is the solution of the problem. Isaac Newton used the metaphor of a hermetically sealed clock to describe the universe – a closed mechanical system, self-contained, with no external environment.

In the last few decades, scientists and thinkers have repudiated the machine metaphor of the world. The mechanistic and fragmented Western view is now replaced by a more organic and holistic Eastern view. It may be described as an *ecological* worldview, where all individual events and actions are not separated but interrelated and interdependent. We are embedded in the never-ending cyclical process of nature.

Paradoxes are curve balls that nature throws at us to get us to pause and re-examine our approach to problem-solving and decision-making. They may come in the form of a statement, proposition, situation or even a person that seems contradictory. These elements are present: two polar opposites, mutual exclusivity and simultaneity. Both claim validity, invoking a sense of absurdity. Our logical understanding of the world is upended. We are gripped by tensions because the contradictions we are faced with defy logic and common sense.

16

Managing contradictions: Chinese vs Western thinking

Discomfort with contradictions is deeply rooted, especially in the Western mind. Aristotelian logic treats contradictions and tensions as signals that the ultimate truth has not been discovered yet. The approach adopted is dialectical thinking, to logically weigh the merits and demerits of both sets of ideas. Once this is done, a single unified truth is discovered. The opposite to this must be wrong. Psychologist Richard Nisbett describes this form of synthesis as "aggressive" because the ultimate goal is to resolve contradictions.

In place of the Western style of logic, the Chinese dialectic uses contradictions to understand relations among objects or events, to transcend or integrate apparent oppositions, or even to embrace colliding viewpoints. Instead of incompatibility, Chinese thinkers see complementarity.

According to Laozi, the Chinese philosopher credited with writing *Dao De Jing*, all things and events in nature are interrelated, connected and are but different manifestations of the same reality. Thus, there is nothing inherently good or bad about opposites in paradoxes. In fact, the Daoists view contradictions as a necessity in life. For one to exist, it needs to have the other. In order to have black, you need to have white. Otherwise, how will you know that you have black?

In Daoism, the two opposing forces are commonly denoted as *yin* and *yang*. The *yin-yang* symbol consists of a circle divided into two fish-shaped halves – much akin to a black dolphin with a white eye intertwining with a white dolphin with a black eye. They represent opposing natural forces coexisting permanently, blending in with each other in a continuous cycle of change.

Let's now look at how one famous Japanese company unleashes creativity through a paradoxical mindset.

Toyota Production System

Toyota has long risen to the highest ranks of the world's best car manufacturers. Behind its success is the famed Toyota Production System (TPS). Though TPS provides a powerful competitive advantage, it does not completely account for Toyota's success. Its secret lies in the power of paradoxes within a culture of contradictions. TPS is a "hard" innovation that drives continuous improvement in the way cars are manufactured. It is complemented by a "soft" innovation that recognizes, nurtures and empowers the humans within the systems.

Toyota started as a humble textile business at the beginning of the 20th century. The founder was Sakichi Toyoda. In 1935, they ventured into car manufacturing. The quality of their cars was poor initially. In 1950, Eiji Toyoda, the founder's son, visited Ford Motor Company in the US to learn from Henry Ford about mass production of cars. After many months, he concluded that the Ford mass manufacturing process did not suit what he had in mind. Ford manufactured one model – the famous Model T – and only in black color. It was Toyoda's aim to produce a variety of cars in one plant.

Faced with financial constraints and labor problems because of the strong Japanese union, he knew that he had to develop an in-house system to realize his manufacturing ambitions. He turned to production engineer Taiichi Ohno, who later developed and perfected the concept of lean manufacturing. It became the Toyota Production System and is seen as the most important technical innovation since Ford's successful implementation of the continuous moving assembly line.

Ohno studied the ideas of Frederick Taylor, the father of scientific management. Taylor believed there were universal principles which governed efficiency in manufacturing, and that these were independent of human judgment. He said, "In our scheme, we do not ask the initiative of our men. We do not want any initiative. All we want of them is to obey the orders we give them, do what we say, and do it quick."

Ohno applied a completely different approach back in Japan. He said, "The Toyota style is not to create results by working hard. It is a system that says there is no limit to people's creativity. People don't go to Toyota to work, they go there to think." Outsiders who eagerly seek to understand the underpinning of Toyota's success will find that it is an enigma. The company succeeds because it has a culture of contradictions. Here are four examples:

1. Toyota manufacturing processes and controls are state-of-the art. Everything is well organized, structured and works like a clock. At the same time, workers are treated with respect and empowered to exercise judgment and take actions they see fit.

2. Though the company has a rigid hierarchy, employees are encouraged to speak up, highlight problems and not blindly obey instructions.

3. Many of Toyota's goals are intentionally vague and ambiguous. This is antithetical to accepted management practices. But many Toyota executives point out the wisdom of painting in broad strokes. When goals are too clearly defined, employees withdraw into the comfort of their own silos to do their own thing. Ambiguity is a powerful impetus to talk across boundaries to explore new avenues of collaboration and exploration.

4. Toyota's development process for new models appears extraordinarily inefficient. Decisions are pushed out as far as possible. But Toyota can turn out new products in much less time than its competitors, a feat that is much admired.

How to navigate organizational paradoxes

There are three common approaches that leaders adopt in navigating paradoxes. Each leads to a different outcome.

Either-or approach: We often don't know what to do with fundamental opposing propositions. Our first impulse is to determine which one has greater merits. This is the either-or approach. Each proposition is analyzed logically and in isolation from the other. One dominates, the other withers. One is right and, therefore, the other is wrong.

Decisions made in this way have the advantage of being quick. In some straightforward situations, it is the ideal way to make a decision. When problems are more complex, however, this way of thinking alienates parties who hold different views, causes polarization, and makes a mockery of critical thinking. It perpetuates an outmoded idea that there is only one truth. Contentions and nuances have no place in the discussions. An example is the statement of the former US President George W. Bush who said after 9/11 at the launch of his anti-terrorism campaign, "Every nation, in every region now has a decision to make. Either you are with us, or you are with the terrorists."

Trade-offs: Still treating the two options as competitive and contradictory, the leader works along the continuum to find where to position the solution. It is through trade-offs that a compromise is struck.

There is also a time and place for this approach. In trying to make a deal with a strong and intransigent party, the only way to move forward may be through trade-offs. But the solution may not be long-term. Both sides may feel that the agreement is lopsided. For example, in the collective bargaining process between workers' union and management, there will inevitably be trade-offs. If mutual trust and a sense of collective destiny are missing, even after the agreement is signed off, the relationship will still remain fraught.

The paradoxical mindset: Instead of considering both alternatives as contradictory, leaders who adopt the paradoxical mindset see them as complementary. The two opposing positions are interdependent. Indeed, one cannot exist without the other. They embrace the tensions to transcend or integrate them. This is a higher order of thinking. It is the *both-and perspective*. In such a worldview, leaders recognize the emergence of multiple truths which together form a whole.

Consider the case of a tech solutions provider. New entrants to the market are posing a major threat. They face the pressure to improve customer service while reducing cost. Their leader reframes the challenge as follows: "What ideas can we think of to achieve both simultaneously?" The team members return within a couple of weeks with a plan to simplify their operating model on customer service. That reduces cost by 30% and improves customer service. The team members themselves realize that what they are doing will only offer a temporary respite as their competitors up their game in response. They set themselves another challenge: offer clients more innovative solutions while maintaining cost competitiveness and improving customer services. Eight months later, they increase their market share considerably.

The next time your team struggle with competing constraints, don't be too quick to turn your attention to providing relief such as allocating more resources or extending the timeline. Instead, reframe it as a creative challenge. When people are faced with seemingly irreconcilable demands, they often surprise themselves with their creativity. Paradoxes, when we learn to embrace them, enable us to transcend self-limiting beliefs imposed by our earlier state of mind.

> *"How wonderful that we have met with a paradox.*
> *Now we have hope of making some progress."*
> Niels Bohr, Nobel Laureate in Physics

It is only in the last few decades that people talk about arts and science in the same sentence. Both disciplines were considered incompatible, with arts and sciences representing the subjective and objective poles of human enterprise. One person who embraced a paradoxical mindset harmonized both brilliantly in his creations. At the launch of iPad 2, Steve Jobs shared the secret to Apple's success: "It's in Apple's DNA that technology alone is not enough — it's technology married with liberal arts, married with the humanities, that yields us the results that make our heart sing."

2

SYSTEMIC THINKING

**Many of today's problems can
only be solved systemically**

*"To develop a complete mind: Study the
science of art; study the art of science.
Learn how to see. Realize that everything
connects to everything else."*
Leonardo da Vinci

VUCA is an acronym frequently used to describe today's business environment. It is short for volatility, uncertainty, complexity and ambiguity. The challenges that we face today can no longer be resolved in the way that most of are used to: break the problem into manageable parts, seek to understand each issue in terms of its symptoms, and apply a fix for that issue. By doing this for all the various symptoms, we think the problem will be fixed. But this will not work for complex problems as there are numerous causes and no simple solutions. And in our haste to move forward, we may focus on the symptoms and introduce measures that may result in unintended consequences. In other words, the cure may be worse than the illness. Here are two cautionary tales.

The story of DDT and Operation Cat Drop
DDT was one of the first chemicals in widespread use as a pesticide. Following World War II, it was promoted as a wonder chemical, the simple solution to pest problems, large and small. Years later, it became apparent

that it inflicted unforeseen harmful effects on the environment, human beings and fish, birds and other forms of wildlife. Today, it is banned in many countries.

In the early 1950s, there was a major outbreak of malaria among the people in Borneo. The World Health Organization (WHO) decided to intervene by spraying large amounts of DDT to eradicate the mosquitoes carrying malaria. Though this succeeded in killing the mosquitoes, WHO had not anticipated the collateral damage that resulted.

One of the first effects was that DDT was also killing a parasitic wasp that ate thatch-eating caterpillars. Without the wasps to eat them, the thatch-eating caterpillars flourished, causing thatched roofs to collapse. Worse than that, the insects that died from being poisoned by DDT were eaten by gecko lizards, which were in turn eaten by cats. The cats started to die, the rats flourished, and the people were threatened by outbreaks of two serious diseases carried by the rats: sylvatic plague and typhus.

To cope with this long chain of unintended consequences, WHO resorted to a rather curious approach. They arranged for a huge number of cats to be parachuted into Borneo to redress the imbalance of a delicate ecological equilibrium. "Operation Cat Drop" was first reported by a British anthropologist, Major Tom Harrison, working in Borneo and Sarawak. His report was widely published in the Western press. It is only fitting that we recall Harrison's advice:

> *"All who wish to do well should repeat this*
> *motto daily: Do good carefully."*

How tiny Qatar ran rings round its giant neighbor Saudi Arabia

For four years, the bitter dispute between Saudi Arabia and its tiny neighbor Qatar simmered on. Then in January 2021, it came to an end with a simple hug in a desert resort. Saudi Crown Prince Mohammed bin Salman embraced Emir Sheikh Tamim bin Hamad Al-Thani, Qatar's head of state.

The rivalry between the two states dates back decades. Essentially it boils down to a test of will between the Saudis, who are the Middle East's pre-eminent power and expect to be treated as such, and the diminutive Qataris, who want to chart their own course. While the Saudis have the weight, the Qataris have the nimbleness.

In June 2017, tensions came to a boil when a group of Gulf sheikhdoms led by Saudi Arabia imposed a total air and commercial blockage on Qatar. Then the Saudi-led coalition laid out 13 conditions on Qatar. They were intended not merely to be as humiliating as possible but also to turn Qatar into a puppet state.

The Qatari ruling family decided that compliance was something that they would never do. Qatar proposed negotiation, which was summarily rejected. In their darkest moments, they found new avenues of sustenance. Diplomatically they cultivated relationships with other friendly Gulf states. Working with Iran, Qatar Airways began serving more destinations than before and became an important source of food imports. They strengthened their defense agreement with Turkey to forestall any invasion. In a show of solidarity, Turkey deployed more troops to their military base in Qatar, and sent cargo ships and hundreds of planes loaded with food to break the blockade.

Qatar not only survived, they emerged more resilient and better prepared for the Covid-19 pandemic that came soon after.

Lessons learned from the DDT and Saudi-Qatar sagas

The examples just cited demonstrate that the traditional problem-solving approach that we have all been taught has severe limitations when tackling complex situations. It is called linear thinking. Linear thinking is cause-and-effect thinking. One cause has one effect. If you want to resolve that effect (also called the symptom), identify that one cause and get it fixed. That should be the end of the problem.

Do refer to the picture below. It is a depiction of the celebrated poem entitled *The Blind Men and the Elephant* by John Godfrey Saxe. This is based on an ancient parable that can be found in Jain, Hindu and

Buddhist scriptures dating as far back as 1500 BCE. Each man is figura-tively blind, as people in organizations tend to be. Individually they focus only on their functional responsibilities, oblivious to their peers' concerns and the interdependencies. Thus, the person who feels the tusk of this huge animal will think that the elephant is a spear. Another who touches the ear is convinced that it is a fan and so on. The result is that they will all be locked in conflict about what the elephant is. Everyone has a frag-mented view, missing out on the complete picture. And so it is with the DDT situation and the Saudi-Qatar standoff.

WHO rightly identified mosquitoes as the carrier of malaria. And malaria destroyed human lives. To stop this effect, mosquitoes must be eradicated. Hence DDT was prescribed. But the full impact of DDT on the ecology in Borneo was not considered at all. WHO also wrongly assumed that DDT would not affect other living things apart from mosquitoes. This unleashed a chain of unintended consequences.

In the case of the Saudi-Qatar confrontation, Saudi Arabia thought that an effective way to bring Qatar to heel would be to overwhelm them with a massive blockage. This powerful display of force would surely snuff the life out of the Qataris. In line with linear thinking, action leads to reaction. The expected reaction was capitulation. But Qatar had ideas of their own. When placed in an existential crisis, they drew upon a complex web of relationships that the Saudi coalition did not or could not foresee. The Saudi action galvanized a series of creative maneuvers by the Qataris.

What is systemic thinking?

Linear thinking is still immensely useful when we are dealing with situations which are predictable and relatively self-contained. For example, your automobile has broken down. To get it up and running will require a certain level of knowledge and expertise. A layman may not be able to do it. Therefore you send it back to an authorized repair agent. Trained and experienced technicians assisted by sophisticated diagnostic software can troubleshoot and identify the underlying causes quite readily. They do it systematically and methodically.

But when the situation you are facing is complex and unpredictable, linear thinking will lead you down the wrong path. As we have seen, linear thinking tends to focus on surface-level behaviors or symptoms. Unfortunately, making a symptom go away won't solve the problem. In fact, it may make things worse and cause trouble elsewhere.

> *"Business and human endeavors are systems...*
> *We tend to focus on snapshots of isolated parts*
> *of the system. And wonder why our deepest*
> *problems never get solved."*
> Peter Senge, Systems Scientist,
> MIT Sloan School of Management

Systemic thinking approaches problems by first asking how various elements within a system – which could be an ecosystem, an organization, or something more dispersed such as a global supply chain – interact with one another. Rather than trying to isolate and tackle individual problems that arise, a systems thinker will wish to understand inter-relationships within the system, look for patterns over time, and seek root causes.

Very often the question is raised about the confusion between thinking "systemically" and "systematically." "Systemically" means to think about the whole system, focusing on the interactions and relationships within the system. "Systematically" means breaking a problem into parts and analyzing it through a logical, disciplined and structured method. In work, we may have to adopt certain processes as laid down by our company. This is being systematic. But it is not what is meant by systemic.

The iceberg model is helpful in understanding the systemic thinking approach. We know that only 10% of its mass is above water while 90% is underwater. But in our behavior at work, our thinking and action are influenced by the 10%. Systems thinking tells us to pay attention to the 90% before making our decisions. Each level down the iceberg offers a deeper understanding of the system being examined as well as increased leverage for changing it.

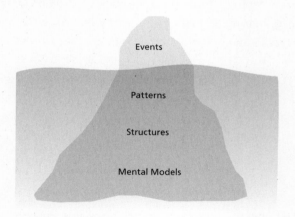

- **Events level:** This the 10% level at which we typically perceive the world. For example, we notice this event happening: two co-workers in a team are frequently disagreeing. We then infer that they are the cause of the team's inability to meet their goals. Or when defective products are coming off an assembly line, we think that it is because it is poorly supervised. The iceberg model reminds us not to jump to such a conclusion as it is only a surface-level observation.

- **Patterns level:** If we look below the events level, we start to see patterns. For example, we notice that the disagreement between the co-workers is related to a few specific issues. Apart from these, they get along well. It is only during shift changes that the number of defective products rises.

- **Structures level:** This relates to the ways parts of a system are organized. Structures include the following in an organization: its hierarchy, the relationship between functions, the power dynamics, policies such as performance targets, rewards and compensation, incentives, rules and regulations, corporate culture, facilities and so on. All these may lead to the events and patterns observed. When roles and responsibilities are ill-defined, co-workers will bicker because they lack clarity. When shift changes take place with no overlap between outgoing and incoming shifts, there's a greater likelihood of defects during such times.

- **Mental models level:** This is related to people's assumptions, beliefs, values and prejudices. In the Saudi-Qatar rivalry, the Saudis could have held the view that Qatar was just too vulnerable to resist. In the unfortunate DDT episode, WHO did not think there would be any side effects from DDT. Or they weren't aware of any, and did not explore further. What if someone in the discussions offered opposing assumptions and beliefs?

Putting it all together
In the next few chapters, we'll discuss several organizational situations that are more effectively handled by taking a systemic approach.

In preparation for this, I would like to suggest that you attempt to apply the iceberg model to recent events that are important and challenging to you. Work your way down the iceberg from events, patterns, structures and finally to mental models. Do not rush. Observe, reflect and seek different perspectives. Having a few trusted colleagues to bounce ideas off will be beneficial. Be prepared to revisit your inferences at every level again and again. After you complete the exercise, ask yourself how your understanding of the situation has deepened as you recognize interconnection between seemingly unrelated aspects of the situation. Are there more holistic approaches that you can consider that didn't occur to you previously?

3

RESOLVING CONFLICT SYSTEMICALLY

Moving from blame to accountability

*"To be effective in the midst of change, leaders must be
able to step back out of the moment and assess what is
happening from a wider perspective. It is called getting
off the dance floor and onto the balcony."*
Ron Heifetz, Harvard University

Whenever something goes wrong in an organization, the first question
that people ask is, "Whose fault is it?" This is a natural reflex when individuals are interacting with each other. But by starting with assigning
blame, minds become closed, curiosity ceases and the parties involved
are more concerned about covering up their errors than seeking a more
complete understanding of the whole situation. As silo-thinking becomes
reinforced and finger-pointing intensifies, the atmosphere is highly
charged. This will be yet another blow to the espoused intention to collaborate and be creative.

A few years ago, the project team of a high-tech company providing
solutions to the automotive and power semiconductor industry faced a
crisis. A key client, an enterprise-level account no less, threatened to pull
the plug on the project after 12 months. Deliverables were not being
met, the timeline was slipping and cost was creeping up.

The project team comprised functions led by two different managers: engineering and product development. The two managers could not see eye to eye with each other on roles and responsibilities. There was an absence of trust and goodwill. Communication was purely transactional. Their mutual antipathy infected team members, who withdrew into their separate silos. The managers had reporting lines to two separate VPs. Though the VPs were fully aware of the tension within the project team, they both kept their distance. It was widely known throughout the company that they had a long history of difficulties with each other. Each VP felt that the issue rested squarely with the other VP. All that they were willing to do was to urge their respective managers to sort out the difficulties with the other party.

As pressure mounted, in exasperation the two managers finally decided to sit down and sort things out with each other. Though the meeting was tense initially, they soon realized that they had to find a better way of working together. They acknowledged that if the project failed, they would both be held accountable. By the end of the session, both were more at ease. The following day, they brought all members of the team together and committed to collaboration. In a couple of meetings over a few hours, all the pent-up emotions and ill feelings seemed to have vaporized.

But their elation was short-lived. Within a month, animosity and finger-pointing resumed. It required a call from the client to HQ to send shock waves down the organization. Now the two VPs were told in no uncertain terms that if they didn't sort things out within a month, they would both become history.

Traditional approaches to conflict resolution

What we have just witnessed is the traditional approach to conflict resolution. It tends to focus on interpersonal tensions instead of exploring the larger systemic issues. By bounding the discussions in this manner, we limit organizational learning and may miss finding a long-term resolution. This was the trap that the managers of the project team fell into. When the context becomes complex, involving many players at different levels in a matrixed organization, there is a need for a more systemic view of conflict.

In the previous chapter, the iceberg model was used to explain systemic thinking. What didn't work with the process adopted by the managers was that it failed to address a whole host of other influences and interfaces that might have led to the difficulties encountered. The two managers implicitly assumed that if they communicated more openly and frequently, the team members would be able to get coordinated and collaborate more harmoniously. Referring to the iceberg model, we could see that their thinking was influenced by the event at the tip of the iceberg: interpersonal conflict. This was in fact a symptom of the complex web of relationships and interdependences involving members of the project team. By focusing their energy on tackling this symptom, the real problem continued to fester.

Taking a systemic approach to conflict

Now that HQ was putting the onus on the two VPs, they finally met and agreed to put their differences aside and get to the bottom of the challenges. They also asked for help from their L&D (Learning & Development) Director. A series of interviews were conducted with the VPs, the managers and the members of the project team. The L&D team also spoke to other functions as well the members of the client team.

Their findings per the steps in the iceberg model were as follows:

Events
- The two managers weren't on the same page
- A lot of disagreement

Patterns
- No shared objectives for the whole team
- Lack of trust
- Sporadic and transactional communication

Structures
- Two separate sub-teams instead of one unified team
- The two VPs weren't in sync and played no part in uniting the two parts of the team
- The two managers had conflicting Key Performance Indicators

Mental models
- Siloed thinking
- Each sub-team viewed the other sub-team as the source of the problem

After the L&D team completed their investigation, they shared their findings with the two VPs and the members of the project team. Their conclusion: the team's lack of collaboration and mistrust resided at the levels of structures and mental models.

It is the primary responsibility of senior leaders to create the conditions for success for the people throughout the organization. It is incumbent on them to provide clarity on context and the definitions of success. For projects involving multiple functions, there must be emphasis on shared goals and collective accountabilities. There needs to be an open dialogue regarding roles and responsibilities for individual work units, as well as their complementarities and interdependencies. The two VPs should role-model the behavioral norms expected of team members. In the matrix reporting model that is now prevalent, members of a project team report into different functions and bosses. If these bosses do not see eye to eye and are at odds with each other, invariably their people will develop troubled relationships with each other. The company's culture plays a key role as well, including its rewards and recognition plan.

Most organizational conflict has its roots in poorly defined expectations, misaligned goals, unclear roles, weak leadership, lack of shared purpose, ineffective communication, absence of trust and psychological safety. These then lead to ill-defined ways of working – meetings, decision-making and the managing of differences of opinion.

Companies need to invest in building a culture of collaboration that gives members a sense of shared purpose and esprit de corps. Each sub-unit or person must see themselves as part of the larger whole. Their first priority is meeting the company's overall goals. Individual KPIs are important of course but must be aligned with their shared purpose. Key conditions for collaboration will include team leadership, psychological safety, well-defined ways of working and ongoing open communications. Giving and receiving feedback must happen frequently and spontaneously so that everybody is aware of their performance and areas for improvement. Employees not only receive training on technical skills but on "soft skills" such as self-awareness, leading without authority, emotional intelligence and so on. Conflicts need not be negative if people know how to manage and harness them for the greater good of the teams. In Chapter 9 we will discuss how to create a high-performance team culture.

Lessons and actions from this incident

The founders of the company were all engineers. They had done well in the last 30 years in focusing on technology. Theirs was a top-down data-driven culture with an overweening focus on getting things done. But not on creating a climate of empowerment, collaboration, openness and trust. The threat of losing a major account jolted them out of their individual silos, right from the top. This was a wakeup call that was long overdue. True to form, they reacted quickly and were able to turn the situation around within three months. Top management committed to embarking on a journey of cultural transformation.

Their biggest learning was that the linear thinking approach that engineers love can't resolve issues involving people interactions. They are just too complex. The systemic thinking approach is now a mandatory topic in the L&D curriculum. Everybody has a role in the company's success. This can only happen if they shift their mindset from blame to accountability. When this becomes part of their culture, it will lead to a more human-centered approach in collaboration.

4

INFLUENCING
WITHOUT
AUTHORITY

Your ideas can't travel unless others support them

*"The only way on earth to influence other people is to talk
about what they want and show them how to get it."*
Dale Carnegie

In today's fast-changing and dynamic business environment, the ability to influence others without relying upon positional authority is vital to leadership success. The days of managers getting people to do what they want them to do by virtue of their position are long gone. More and more companies are achieving global scale, embracing flatter management and matrix reporting structures that reduce traditional hierarchies and utilize cross-functional teams. Leaders need to find more effective ways of securing buy-in and commitment than simply resorting to formal authority that is linked to their titles.

There is a growing trend that many people have huge responsibilities, carry titles such as manager or even director, and do not directly oversee anybody. But for all intents and purposes, they are leaders. The way they get things done will be via their ability to influence others.

In global, and indeed regional business teams, tensions frequently erupt when financial numbers are not met. Some time ago, a regional business leader found herself mired in a conflictual relationship between her three country managers and the director of supply chain. A couple of country managers attributed their poorer results to delays in order fulfilment by supply chain.

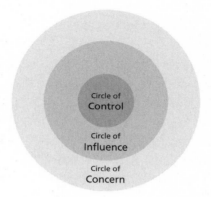

It was the typical silo thinking in action. Of the three country managers, two viewed their responsibilities as circumscribed by their circle of control. Outside this was an ill-defined circle of influence that involved managing relationships with other peers. This was however complicated by the competing priorities of various stakeholders that went into the circle of concern. The two country managers felt they weren't getting the attention from supply chain due to their lack of formal authority. Hence it was up to their boss to sort things out with the head of supply chain.

But Jess, the third country manager, who was also facing the heat to raise her team's performance, embraced a higher perspective. She intuitively accepted that as a senior leader she had to expand her circle of influence. Operating within a self-imposed and imaginary cocoon of control would be self-defeating in this complex and interconnected world. At her pay grade, it was incumbent upon her to purposefully wade into the circle of concern. This was where she could engage her peers collaboratively to resolve company-wide challenges. And that was what she applied herself to. In the months ahead, she and her team made great strides in spite of challenging market dynamics. What did Jess do that her two other peers couldn't?

The six principles of influencing

To be effective influencers, leaders need to develop strong relationships, establish their credibility, and learn about the goals, priorities and values of others to form the basis for future influencing strategies. Good leaders understand that laying this foundation is critical, making it possible for them to convince people to change their behaviors, consider new options, or support new initiatives. In general, these requests are more likely to be followed when leaders know how to adopt and tailor six key principles of persuasion:

1. Relationship. Put yourself in the shoes of the individual or group of people you are trying to influence. Why should they be open to you and your suggestions if they don't know you? What if you already had a good and mutually trusting relationship with them?

As human beings, it is natural for us to be more willing to lend a listening ear to someone we know than someone who is a complete stranger. Therefore it is always a good habit to reach out and get to know others in the organization. Instead of communicating through email, arrange to talk to each other face-to-face if possible. The second option is to do a video call. The third is to have a phone call. Look for opportunities to have a nice informal chat over a cup of tea or coffee. Make it a point to keep in touch on an ongoing basis. Building relationships is not a one-shot event.

2. Context. Before seeking to win the support of another party, pause and seek to know more about the context which the other party is in. What are their needs, priorities, constraints and working style? This is of paramount importance. Many a time, they are impacted by factors outside their control, such directives set by their bosses and trade-offs they may have to make to get things done. We frequently gloss over these in our haste to get things done. Without such a contextual understanding, we may start off on the wrong footing because we simply don't know enough about their world. If we are lucky, we may get a non-committal response. In the worst case, we turn that person off. This is definitely frustrating and embarrassing.

3. Common ground. It's easier to build consensus when people share common goals as everyone will invariably have different KPIs. A common purpose serves as a foundation for negotiation and cooperation. Appealing to these goals will make any influencing strategy far more effective.

Beyond this, it is necessary to have an overview of the dynamics in the larger environment. Seek to understand how all the functions and parts of the organization fit together. Across organizations, misalignment, friction and fragmentation are common. These result in pain points. Every function has such pain points. Here is a good segue to add value and gain trust: Go the extra mile to help build coalition among those who are disconnected from each other. It's really at the intersection of the various parts of the organization that transformation can happen

Jess, the country manager, viewed the problem that she and her two other colleagues were encountering from a systemic perspective. This was an ongoing bone of contention between the country managers and supply chain. She decided that no headway would be made if all parties dug in their heels. She thought about this over the weekend and decided to depersonalize the conflict by viewing the conflict as though she were a third party, putting some distance between herself and the situation. When she approached the supply chain director, she had no preconceived notion about how to solve the long-running complaint about order fulfilment. But she did know that the fraught relationship between the country managers and the supply chain was spreading across the whole company like a virus, dragging others unwillingly into the conflict. This had to stop. She sought to understand the difficulties faced by the supply chain organization. Then she shared the challenges from the country managers' angle. Soon after, she initiated a four-way video call involving the two country managers, the supply chain team and herself. It took many sessions over two months. They all agreed to keep their boss posted on what they were doing collectively. But their request was that the boss need not be involved as this was down to them as senior leaders. The breakthrough came when all parties were able to listen and empathize. With that, they agreed on a plan to collaborate with each other so that the whole company benefitted.

If you are a member of a leadership team, chances are there have already been many discussions about the company's overall objectives. If these have been well defined, with every leader providing inputs, they will form the basis of a common ground for collaboration.

4. Credibility. People are more likely to take a request seriously if they respect the expertise and integrity of the person making it. Someone with a track record of success or a reputation for honesty, fairness and professionalism will generally find it easier to use influencing strategies effectively. Their voice will be heard during critical conversations. Trustworthiness is a precious asset to cultivate and possess. It is a key determinant of whether others are willing to consider your suggestions. (See box on the ABCD Trust Model, developed by Ken Blanchard.)

5. Reciprocity. Let's be practical. Everybody is busy and overloaded with work. We are all short of time and there are countless requirements from many stakeholders pulling us in various directions. And everybody will treat their KPIs as their highest priority. In deciding what to focus on, they will invariably do what is in their best interests. This is the WIIFM (What's In it For Me) motive.

Therefore we need to ask ourselves: What will interest the other persons most, i.e. the WIIFT (What's In It For Them) factor.

As an example, one manager in a matrixed organization found himself lacking the resources to develop an app that his department needed. He sought the help of another department which could possibly tag the development of this app onto a software they were working on. He was able to present it as an opportunity for the other department head to make his software even more versatile and useful. And he candidly

The ABCD Trust Model

The ABCD Trust Model explains that there are four factors that determine whether others deem you trustworthy. It starts with an emotional connection (C) that happens instinctively. People either feel comfortable with you or they don't. It is the vibes or energy that you send out. Following closely will be your reputation or track record. Are you known for your ability (A) and dependability(D)? All these will add to your believability (B). It takes a long time for trust to be established. But it can be lost overnight if these ingredients seem no longer present in your behavior subsequently. You may find more about trust-building in Chapter 18.

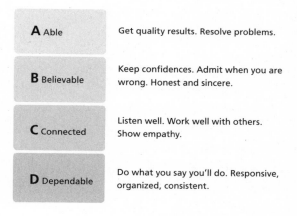

A Able	Get quality results. Resolve problems.
B Believable	Keep confidences. Admit when you are wrong. Honest and sincere.
C Connected	Listen well. Work well with others. Show empathy.
D Dependable	Do what you say you'll do. Responsive, organized, consistent.

admitted upfront that it would help his department better serve some important clients as well.

In another situation, a sales head wrote an email thanking a colleague in another part of the world for delivering a quantity of product that was key to meeting a crucial customer requirement. That colleague had taken an extra effort as it was a trial order, the quantity being very small. He copied her boss on this email. She had bent backwards to provide support to the sales head because she was committed to customer-centricity.

6. Network. In work and in life, we need to network widely. By having connections in the right places, we may be able to call upon influential people who can be of help to us. If we are well connected, people whom we are seeking help from may notice it too. The human mind works this way: "As he knows so many influential persons in our company, it is better for me to be more co-operative." A word of caution: we should not go around flaunting our connections. It can backfire on us.

The right influence strategy

While there are many influencing strategies, four stand out as most effective when attempting to influence without authority:

- **Reasoning:** Use logical arguments and factual evidence to explain why a task is necessary.

- **Connecting emotionally:** Appeal to the person's values and ideals. Create enthusiasm by sharing why this piece of work will further the interests of the company.

- **Collaborating:** Ask, and listen actively, for inputs and suggestions to improve the quality of your proposal and gain buy-in.

- **Helping each other:** Reduce the difficulty of meeting your request by offering to provide relevant resources or assistance. Be willing to compromise.

Putting it all together

Although we have discussed the six principles of influence separately for the sake of clarity, you need to decide how they will be used in combination to compound their impact. Which principles to use more of, and which of the four strategies are more appropriate, is a judgment call you will need to make. Influencing is more an art than a science.

Situational awareness combined with emotional intelligence will be the underpinnings.

Refrain from taking a universal one-size-fits-all approach. All situations are context-dependent. Seeking to harness collaboration is meaningless unless we consider the other parties' goals, values and interest along with the power relationships.

Being able to influence without authority is the currency of effective leadership. Diverse ideas and opposing needs will continue to proliferate and multiply. Such pluralism makes for a vibrant and innovative culture. But it can also lead to dysfunctionality. Leaders need to be willing to step outside their authority, and venture purposefully into ill-defined and ambiguous areas to co-create workable solutions for the organization in the midst of complexity and conflict.

5

THE NECESSARY ART OF POSITIVE POLITICS

Advance your interests without losing your honor and dignity

"Man is by nature a political animal."
Aristotle

A sure way of making people in organizations squirm is to ask them about workplace politics. It is the elephant in the room: everyone knows that it is present, but very few want to openly discuss it. The topic conjures up images of opaqueness in decision-making, backstabbing, sucking up, and playing people against each other.

For instance, some people may fail to secure approval for their projects despite an inordinate amount of hard work. Yet another colleague gets endorsement time and again. In another situation, a division head consistently outperforms in delivering all his business objectives. But when his company acquires a competitor, he is left in the cold while other peers whose performance pales in comparison are given larger roles in the merged entity. What is going on? Are there some unofficial rules or secret handshake that govern the dynamics here? How does one work the system to get ahead?

What is office politics?

The truth is that all organizations are political entities. Why do organizations exist in the first place? Because of the realization and hope that when a group of like-minded people work together, they can achieve much more than a single person working alone. However, interpersonal dynamics can quickly become complicated as people think and behave differently. Though they may sign up to a common vision, each individual will put her own spin to it. Throw into this mix diverse aspirations, motives and values. Voila! You now have conflicting perspectives, and the attendant need for people to influence others to achieve their personal, team or organizational goals. This is office politics.

Being a member of an organization is already a political act. Resources are scarce. Organization structures are flattening. Bosses and peers have their own diverse interests. Those who presume that the powers-that-be will always act rationally and dispassionately are sadly deluded. The politically savvy, however, are clear-eyed about human nature: stakeholders will protect their own needs while pursuing legitimate business objectives. By putting themselves in these stakeholders' shoes, they will discover what these are. Their ideas will stand a higher chance of acceptance if stakeholders recognize that their own needs have been addressed.

The fact is nobody really likes office politics. But it is there. To make an impact in your own organization, like it or not, you're going to need to learn to play the game. That doesn't mean you have to play dirty and lose your soul, but you have to figure out how to influence those around you.

Two real-life cases

Case 1: Viewing organizational dynamics through different lenses.

Consider this scenario. Wen and Rahu are business heads of a European pharmaceutical company based in Hong Kong. In the recent organizational restructure, two key functions traditionally in the commercial division – customer service and technical support – have been centralized under the powerful regional HQ in Shanghai. This is in line with the shift towards matrix reporting. Both leaders have earlier expressed concerns that the restructuring will adversely impact the speed with which key account managers can win critical deals and service clients.

Wen and Rahu are both highly successful and widely respected throughout the company. But people notice unmistakable differences in the way they make sense of complex challenges. While Rahu treats conflict, ambiguity and power dynamics as a technical matter, Wen takes a nuanced approach. He views things through multiple lenses and makes greater meaning out of them. Developmental psychologists call this *meaning-making* capability.

Wen is always calm and measured in his response. He values collaboration, and invests in building relationships within and outside the company. He sizes up situations fast, and definitely has a point of view. But he will listen, study the lay of the land and then adapt accordingly. When he interacts with any colleague, he seeks to appreciate the web of relationships that he's in that may facilitate or hamper his intentions or actions. He has always counselled colleagues that it is sometimes better to lose a battle in order to win the war.

Rahu is described as passionate, driven and principled. He is self-confident and very decisive. He possesses much deeper knowledge of the business than any other leader in the company. As such, once his mind is made up on a certain course of action, he will not budge. Technical mastery is both his strength and weakness.

A year after the reorganization, Wen and his team have adapted themselves to the new realities. Wen's intensified effort to strengthen relationships with the regional HQ is paying off. With the latter's support, he embraces customer service and technical support as his business partners. As the partnership deepens, he has pre-empted the silo thinking that he had feared. They have become a high-performance team with a common purpose. His business is growing at a fast clip, far exceeding expectations. Bosses hold their partnership as an exemplar of cross-functional collaboration at its best.

In contrast, Rahu and his team are struggling. As anticipated, the wall goes up as soon as regional HQ takes charge of customer service and technical support. Misalignment and differing priorities become manifest. In the midst of his troubles, he still harks back to the days when all was under him and things could turn on a dime.

Case 2: Getting passed over for promotion. Jack is tall and athletic. He speaks animatedly and has a warm personality. People who work with him at all levels speak highly of him because of his approachability and ability to stay unruffled in tough situations. In terms of execution, his results are outstanding. He and his team have met or surpassed their numbers in each of the last three years. It is therefore a disappointment for him when the company announces that his co-worker Elaine will be promoted to vice president instead.

He isn't entirely blindsided by the announcement. The previous week, his boss spoke to him about his decision to give the job to Elaine. He assured Jack that he had a great future with the company, and by developing in a couple of areas he would be ready for advancement. The comments were rather vague, such as developing executive presence and expanding his network in the company. Comments such as these aren't specific enough and represent an information void. Yet many bosses will say similar things. There is a discomfort about delivering explicit feedback for fear of losing a good employee. Jack senses that he isn't getting the full story.

He decides to find out more, and approaches his boss's boss. Before this, he asks his boss whether he will be fine with this. To his surprise, his boss agrees readily. In looking back, clearly his direct boss was only too happy to have a higher-level manager do the tough work for him. The senior leader is forthright in his feedback: Jack has been too busy working with his team and neglecting the building of strategic relationships. As a result, very few executives at HQ know Jack. Elaine in contrast has not only delivered stellar results like Jack but has demonstrated her ability to think strategically and influence leaders far above her. Such criteria for promotion to VP aren't always clearly spelt out. If Jack had stepped away a little from the daily grind and asked himself what it would take to be VP, he would have decoded the so-called unwritten rules for himself.

Politics: Positive and negative

Positive and negative politics are the *yin-yang* of organization life. Whether it is considered positive or negative will be determined by the means deployed, and goals desired. These are the bright and dark ends of a spectrum along which people have to choose how they wish to play the political game.

Negative politics is about advancing oneself by any means necessary. These including hurting others, being unscrupulous, and jeopardizing overall interests. The goals are self-serving. The working climate becomes toxic as people feel victimized and helpless when hidden forces are manipulating who gets what, when, how.

Positive politics, on the other hand, focuses on maximizing and leveraging relationships in order to achieve organizational, team and individual goals. The means used include legitimate ways of getting the attention of powerful people, managing stakeholders, networking, influencing with and without authority, and building alliances. It may even be necessary to engage in some "I'll support your proposal if you do the same for mine" deals. Quid pro quo is part and parcel of human interaction. There is nothing wrong with advancing one's career as long as it also serves the organizational interest.

People who practice positive politics are vigilant and street smart. Through their network, they keep abreast with what is happening. When they sense that a political spear is about to be hurled in their direction, they will not be caught unawares. They will respond appropriately. When necessary, they will not flinch from exercising a sharp elbow. Such leaders are a force for good. They are custodians of a healthy and optimistic business climate in which people collaborate for a better future. In fact, they aren't even deemed to be political at all.

"I am increasingly convinced that people who have power are not necessarily smarter than others. Beyond a certain level of intelligence and level in the hierarchy, everyone is smart. What differentiates people is their political skills and savvy."
Jeffrey Pfeffer, Professor,
Stanford Graduate School of Business

Developing political skills

Gerald Ferris and his colleagues at Florida State University have done much research about political savvy at work. When "properly applied," they say, "it makes good things happen, both for those who use it and for the organizations in which they work." They have shown that politically skilled leaders are masters of four practices:

1. **Social astuteness:** This refers to leaders' ability to recognize social cues within an organizational context. Such individuals demonstrate a high level of self- and contextual-awareness in social settings, sensing the emotions in the environment and what drives people within it.

2. **Interpersonal influence:** This represents the leaders' adaptability when seeking to engage and persuade others to their cause. They devote time to understanding their stakeholders' needs and agenda. They then customize their message to ensure that their impact is optimized.

3. **Networking ability:** This is crucial as it gives leaders access to vital information and opportunities. Leaders with a rich and diverse network can help others succeed as they can point them to new contacts and resources.

4. **Sincerity:** In the course of interaction, how sincere the leaders come across will be a crucial factor. Leaders must be genuine, consistent, and congruous in what they say and do. It is also through this that trust will be built.

Three additional practices may be useful to inculcate:

1. **Decoding the hidden rules of engagement:** This is where we circle back to the notion of unofficial rules in decision-making. Rules do exist but are hidden from plain sight. They are embedded in the corporate culture which guides the ways things are done in the company. Every company has its own unique culture. A high-flying executive in one company may flounder when parachuted into the C-suite of another company.

2. **Finding out who the influencers are:** Influence and power come from various sources: title, formal authority, connections, expertise, or a long history with the company. These are the people who can help you become successful, and you want them on your side. Mapping out your key stakeholders will be an indispensable first step. Such people can help you decode the corporate culture.

3. **Building a solid reputation:** This cannot be over-emphasized, as it is the foundation upon which you reach out and interact with others. How credible and respected are you? Are you optimistic, collaborative and willing to listen to others? Do people trust you? Do your actions match your words? How do you show up to the people who know you?

Pervasiveness of office politics

There are numerous surveys done in many parts of the world that have highlighted the prevalence of office politics. In a 2016 survey by staffing firm Accountemps, 80% of the respondents said office politics exists in their offices, 55% mentioned that they take part in office politics, and 28% felt that politicking is very necessary to get ahead. A 2017 Roffey Park survey covering working life in Singapore, Hong Kong and China identified politics within organizations as a key source of dissatisfaction and a major stressor.

Office politics is a permanent fixture in our working life. Political innocents will find organizations to be rather inhospitable places. By ignoring the political landscape they are handicapping themselves in their career trajectory. Despite their talents and contribution, they will not get the recognition and the influence that they deserve. Their powerlessness will be felt by all. Even their team members who need them to provide aircover in political skirmishes will feel that their flanks are exposed.

While the dark side of politics is a key factor to contend with, most organizations are not pathologically political. Mostly the setbacks are caused by a lack of political skills which are crucial for corporate survival and success. Challenges are almost never purely technical. By viewing them through different lenses, more useful insights can be gathered. Leaders who are politically savvy will enhance their stature and influence, and lead their organizations more effectively while advancing their career.

6

FEWER, SMARTER AND BETTER MEETINGS

Free up cognitive bandwidth for meaningful work

*"If left unchecked, no one will have the time
to get any work done. This is why everyone plays
catch-up after hours and on weekends."*
Michael Mankins, Bain & Company

There are three truths about meetings in organizations. First, they take up a lot of managerial time at all levels, typically about 40%–90% of available hours. Second, the cost in terms of lost productivity is enormous, yet it remains hidden and unaccounted for. And third, meetings continue to proliferate mindlessly, and no one feels able to stop them.

Here are some frequently heard comments:

- Meetings are seen as thieves of time. People get frustrated. They resort to coming in early and leaving later to catch up on work.
- Senior leaders who initiate the meetings lament the wastefulness of meetings.
- Every meeting chaired by a senior leader will result in three or four more down the ranks, involving countless other employees.

- Because managers don't have quiet time to think and plan, they make poor decisions. These translate into unnecessary and counter-productive work for others. More meetings are called to redress these, creating a vicious cycle.
- Managers at all levels behave like good corporate citizens. They resent the tyranny of meetings but will put up with them.

Must you and your colleagues accept this as your fate in organizations? I think not. I have worked with many companies that struggled helplessly with this until it dawned upon the executive leadership teams that they could do something about it. They had allowed wasteful meetings to take over their work days, sucking out oxygen and quality time for reflection, thinking and collaboration. Absent these, ill-conceived strategies were rushed into implementation. Though they communicated with the rest of the company about the "what," scant details were provided about the "how" and the "'why." This became a recipe for confusion, misalignment, poor execution and endless fire-fighting.

Despite the litany of statistics and comments about bad meetings, it is unrealistic to abolish meetings. Well-conducted meetings can bring together ideas and opinions, and allow people to do their job in a more aligned and collaborative manner. They can help establish and promote a common purpose, thus serving as a focal point for collective drive. The solution is not no meetings. But fewer, smarter and better meetings.

Types of meetings

Broadly speaking, there are five types of meetings that are useful:

1. Meetings to solve problems, make decisions and define actions
2. Business and project review meetings
3. Dissemination of information such as all-hands meetings
4. Planning meetings
5. One-on-one meetings such as between a manager and a direct report or between two co-workers

As problem-solving, decision-making and taking actions constitute the lifeblood of organizations, let's focus on such meetings. The ideas discussed, however, will be applicable to the other types of meetings.

A systemic approach to managing meetings

You and your organization need not be held captive by meeting madness. Here is a systemic approach to free up bandwidth for productive work. You can't do it individually. It must be done collectively, starting from the top. There are two phases in this systemic approach.

- Phase 1: Analyzing and changing the pattern of meetings
- Phase 2: Inculcating a new meeting protocol

Phase 1: Analyzing and changing the pattern of meetings

I recommend that once the senior leadership team commit to tackling the meeting problem as a key priority, one member can volunteer and step up as a gatekeeper. A gatekeeper represents the whole leadership team to coordinate and oversee the proper conduct of an important activity. The whole leadership team are still the owners of the meeting problem. But it makes for a balanced distribution of responsibility for members to take turns to be gatekeepers and engage the whole team for further deliberation. Slaying the meeting dragon is intricate and will require concerted effort on a number of fronts. One gatekeeper can't do it all.

The five basic steps are:

1. Identify the types of meetings. Senior leaders can work together to compile a list of meetings that they themselves attend or initiate. What are the purposes and the cadences? Who are the hosts? Ask for estimates of time spent and the people involved. How useful are such meetings? Go down a few levels and do the same. The gatekeeper will define a timeline for this activity.

2. Review and interpret the data. The gatekeeper will lead a review of the data. Such a review will identify meetings which overlap or are unproductive. Agree on what actions to take to streamline or eliminate certain meetings. Sharing the findings with other parts of the organization such as HQ and other regions will be necessary. HQ, for instance, may be responsible for numerous meetings which take up an inordinate amount of time. They are usually oblivious to the impact of such meetings on the well-being of their geographically dispersed colleagues.

For example, if the HQ is located in the US, invariably global meetings will be timed to take place in the morning, say, in Austin, Texas. This will be close to midnight in China and mid-afternoon in the UK. Typically, APAC-based people will have to stay awake till 2 am for each video call. It will disrupt their sleeping pattern, with chronic effects on their physical, mental and emotional health. I have seen instances where one senior US leader insensitively requested 50 APAC employees to attend his briefing scheduled at 11 am his time. This is midnight in China and 1 am in Japan. A pain-sharing arrangement is more equitable, i.e. scheduling the meetings so that all three regions take turns to stay up late for the meetings.

3. Agree on collective goals and outcomes of meetings. Senior leaders need next to define the collective goals and outcomes for the various types of meetings to be conducted. These are to be shared and communicated throughout the organization for further inputs and to achieve buy-in.

4. Set milestones and monitor progress. As with all change efforts, concrete and measurable progress needs to be assessed and tracked regularly. In one company, senior leaders soon find that they have more time throughout the week to reflect and think further ahead. They also notice that their team members are visibly less caught up in meetings. The number of attendees at meetings is halved in some cases. Overall, there are fewer but better meetings.

5. Debrief at six-monthly intervals. For the first 18 months, it is important to take stock of the impact of the new meeting pattern on the workforce. Do a poll on whether people are now experiencing a reduction in the time spent at meetings. By how much? How useful are the meetings they are attending? What has gone well? What can be improved? How is the freed-up time being put to better use? Managers should make it a point to check in with their people regularly. HR business partners may render valuable inputs here.

There is an unintended consequence that may occur. When meeting time is reduced, managers may still find that their calendars continue to get filled up. If they are now consciously working on important matters that they never found time for previously, it is perfectly fine. But this may not be the case. In many companies, every person's calendar is accessible online, so other people may rush in and book their time when an open slot appears. It pays to be mindful about this. Otherwise, it is back to square one.

Phase 2: Inculcating a new meeting protocol

There are four steps in this phase:

1. Adopt a steward's mindset. This starts with senior leaders leading the way by role-modelling the mindset of a time steward. This can be a keystone habit for the company. A keystone habit is a behavior that creates a domino effect which positively impacts other processes. For instance, by exercising regularly, you become healthier, sleep better, and become more alert and effective in life and work.

In October 1987, Paul O'Neill was newly appointed as CEO of Alcoa, the aluminum manufacturing giant. Alcoa's product lines were faltering, profit margins and revenue were in decline. And though their safety record was better than other American companies', it was not good enough. An industry outsider, O'Neill stunned investors and employees by not speaking about how he would turnaround the company. He chose to focus on safety: making Alcoa the safest company in America. This was a keystone habit that galvanized Alcoa. It led to other sweeping process improvements across the whole company. When he retired 13

56

years later, Alcoa's annual earnings were five times higher than when he started.

If you wish to break the vicious cycle of bad meetings, first cultivate a keystone habit. In this instance it is to adopt the time steward's mindset. In holding any meetings, be very mindful that the attendees are putting their time and energy at your disposal. It is your obligation to ensure that they extract value out of the meetings. The steward's mindset can be practiced by everyone in the company, whether she carries the title of manager or not. The effect will of course be much more powerful if top leadership leads the way.

2. Pre-meeting preparation. Before initiating any meeting, pause and consider the following:

- Q1: Why do I need to have this meeting? If it's a virtual meeting, what else must be considered?
- Q2: What are the desired objectives?
- Q3: What will success look like when we achieve these objectives?
- Q4: Who needs to be involved? And why?
- Q5: What is the role of each attendee?
- Q6: What must go into the agenda so that everyone comes fully prepared?

If you can't convincingly answer these six questions, you shouldn't have the meeting. Preparation will require time. And indeed it should. High-quality preparation will result in shorter and more productive meetings.

Develop a detailed agenda with time allocation. Break away from the usual itemized list. Instead of short phrases such as "Outsourcing production of Omega Plus," pose question(s) to be answered, e.g. "Under what conditions should we outsource the production of Omega Plus?" This stimulates thinking and clarifies what will be discussed. It will be useful to ask attendees for inputs. This will enroll them as co-owners of the meeting.

It is always wise to minimize the number of attendees. In many companies, a meeting invitation is seen as a sign of one's importance and prestige. The host must make hard choices: no spectators.

Jeff Bezos has a two-pizza rule. If you need more than two pizzas to feed everyone, you have too many participants. Michael Mankins, a leading researcher on how companies waste time, has what he calls a Rule of Seven for decision-making meetings. For every additional participant beyond seven, the likelihood of making a sound decision reduces by 10%. By the time, you get to 17 people, the chances of your actually making a decision are zero.

3. Hosting and facilitating. Being the host, always arrive early. Greet and welcome attendees and thank them for being punctual. Start strongly about the purpose of the meeting. Introduce attendees who may be new or do not know each other. I recommend a personal check-in at the start (see box). Remind all on previously agreed-upon rules of engagement such as keeping comments to the point, taking turns to speak and being receptive to differing opinions. As the host, do recognize that it is your responsibility to steer the meeting in the right direction. It will mean that you need to exercise control, albeit with a light touch.

Make the first topic "Review and modify the agenda as needed." Slow down and invite comments. Silence may not mean attendees have nothing to add. They are just warming up and getting ready to speak. Wait patiently. Next discuss and seek alignment on the desired objectives of the meeting, and what success will look like. Are the needs and expectations of every participant considered?

To get people to be fully engaged, discourage Powerpoint presentations as far as possible. Ask attendees to put their views succinctly in the form of a narrative. Our brains process good storytelling much better than charts and hard data. If someone feels that she has some background information to share as pre-reading, she can prepare a short note. Give participants a few minutes to do silent reading. As the conversation starts, adopt the steward's mindset. Ask questions to model curiosity

The personal check-in

This is a great ritual to practice before every meeting. It doesn't take a lot of time – just about 15 minutes. It's a good way to foster psychological safety and put people at ease. If they have something important to say in the presence of all, not giving them that time will put a damper on their spirit for the rest of the meeting.

I noticed this when I was observing two group sessions a few months ago. The leader of the first group spent 20 minutes on the personal check-in. The leader of the second group dispensed with it in the interest of time. In any case, they all knew each other, he reasoned.

The difference in the quality of interactions between the two groups was stark. Group 1 participants were lively and animated. They had a very productive meeting with lots of interactions and new ideas offered. As for Group 2, they seemed disengaged and not connected with each other. A private chat with some participants revealed that a few of them felt excluded about a major decision made in the previous month. As they didn't get to share it upfront, it weighed on their mind heavily throughout the meetings.

To conduct the check-in, ask each person to take turns to share their thoughts while the rest listen with empathy. The leader should participate as well, but be the last to speak. Try this and experience its magic. People are more energized, feel included and participate more spontaneously. This works even in virtual sessions.

and active listening, draw out concerns and encourage the quieter participants to voice their opinions. Create an atmosphere for everybody to speak up without fear. This happens only when there is psychological safety.

I have noticed that decision-making meetings frequently drag on and on because parties involved are debating the topic for the first time. A good practice to adopt is for those who have a vested interest in a particular decision to meet before the session to hash things out. This must of course be done with transparency. Have a rigorous discussion of the key issues, sparing no important details, and seek to reach an agreement that all are comfortable with. During the meeting proper, do provide a summary and the recommended solution. Other participants can of course raise questions and offer different perspectives as they see fit.

The importance of a robust decision-making process cannot be overestimated and must not be glossed over. Otherwise, there may be an illusion of consensus. But no ownership and follow-through. Please see Chapter 8.

Finally, the wrap-up. Who will take what actions? By when? This is recorded in a one-pager, and will act as a meeting summary. Remember to end the meeting on time.

4. The follow-up. The one-pager should be distributed to all attendees within a day or two. The expectation is that assignments are completed on time. Attendees can prompt each other as many tasks require interdependent and complementary activities.

Fewer, smarter and better meetings

Phases 1 and 2 working in concert have helped many organizations break out of the trap of endless unproductive meetings. Phase 1 sets a framework which can be revised and improved as needed. Phase 2 goes beyond its impact on meeting protocol. As a keystone habit it can be transformational. People now understand that they are the custodians of the company's most valuable resources: time and the collective energy of colleagues. When you act as a steward of others' time, it's an act of thoughtfulness and care. The ripple effect will continue. People will pay it forward and be inspired to treat others with respect and consideration. Your organization will soon reap the virtuous cycle of greater job satisfaction, higher productivity and people engagement.

7

MAKING TIME MANAGEMENT AN ORGANIZATIONAL PRIORITY

Beyond a personal responsibility, companies must address it institutionally

"Time is the scarcest resource, and unless it is managed nothing else can be managed."
Peter Drucker

The higher leaders move up the organization, the greater will be the pressure and complexity of their roles. And they will face the acute scarcity of one resource: time. There is never enough time to do what should be done. How time is managed will be a major determinant of their own effectiveness and the performance of their organization. Ironically, though, most managers, at all levels, are poor time managers.

Even more pernicious is their lack of understanding that the people who work for them are just as hard-pressed for time. Like their bosses up there, they are overworked. Consider the following two cases:

Case 1: A few years ago, a critical strategic initiative of a multinational stalled. This was one among many that were rolled out in the midst of a major restructuring in the company. The CEO was acutely aware that it was a very busy time for all. But as he and the executive leadership team put it, "Failure is not an option."

In an effort to restart the stalled project, the decision was to assign a talented, up-and-coming General Manager, Amelio from Latin America, to take charge. As it would leave a void in the senior leadership ranks in Latin America, they further decided that this upstanding leader would double-hat: be responsible for his current role while overseeing the project. There was only one problem. Amelio was already working 18-hour days. With this additional workload, he would have to forgo sleep completely.

Case 2: Susan is the business head of a financial services firm based in Singapore. She oversees a team of financial and investment analysts in ASEAN, China and Japan. Since her promotion into this role a year ago, it's been a frenzy of activities. Her team managers leading each of the three regions keep her very busy by involving her in all their operational and review meetings. She really doesn't mind as she loves to deep-dive into details and feel the pulse of the business. It has always been her modus operandi.

But something is troubling her now. She feels it in her guts. In the endless swirl of activities, she sees herself getting sucked deeper into the trenches. While this is happening, the team managers are at the periphery looking on rather than taking charge. Is she pulling her weight as a business head? The feedback from her Regional Vice President at the recent review is a wakeup call: "You need to get yourself out of the weeds. Stop doing things that your team managers should be doing. At your pay grade, the time spent should be aligned with our strategic priorities."

Time management goes far beyond personal discipline
The two cases illustrate the symbiotic relationship between organizational priorities and time management by individuals. In Case 1, the CEO was willfully oblivious to the workload of the people lower down

the organization. Initiative overload on top of new strategic directions and reorganization made it impossible for individuals like Amelio to time manage. In Case 2, Susan withdrew into her comfort zone by focusing on operational matters that were best delegated to her team leaders. She lacked the discipline to focus her time and energy on strategic issues.

Time is the scarcest resource of any organization. While it is expected that individuals are responsible for managing their time effectively, factors within the corporate structure have powerful influences that will stymie their best intentions and efforts.

To avoid squandering this finite resource, companies should manage time more systemically. There are two phases in this systemic approach, starting at senior levels before cascading downwards:

- Phase 1: Create time budget and formal processes for allocating their time
- Phase 2: Ensure individuals prioritize their time in alignment with company priorities

Phase 1: Create time budget and formal processes for allocating time

There is generally a blind spot at HQ. Top leaders treat leadership bandwidth down the ranks as a limitless resource. This is a far cry from the discipline of financial management in which formal approval is required for expenses, headcounts, capital expenditure. Companies need to make a mindset shift. Start treating time like financial capital, as scarce and limited. This is another keystone habit (see Chapter 6).

In numerous consulting assignments with leadership teams, I have noticed that in the regions away from HQ, the staff can barely keep their heads above water, juggling between managing the business and the proliferation of big strategic initiatives coming from above. This is an endless struggle between HQ and regions, with the latter suffering in silence. The net result is "change fatigue," with a variety of unintended consequences, including failed initiatives, missed opportunities and subpar business results. Leaders don't have time to engage the frontline staff who are customer-facing. Strategic and operational matters are both left unattended, because HQ makes relentless calls on their time. Eventually, people get confused and demoralized.

> *"Time is a finite resource. Before you ask for something new to be added, decide what must be subtracted."*

I know of a few companies that have established a governance committee with a remit to oversee and monitor the "leadership bandwidth" for enterprise-wide initiatives. This committee has an overview of time availability for leaders three levels down from the CEO for driving new initiatives. Before any new initiatives are approved, proposals must include time commitments and whether current leaders have the available bandwidth.

If this process had been adopted, the company in Case 1 would have taken a different approach with that critical initiative that later ground to a halt. For sure, they would not have foisted the stalled initiative onto Amelio, a key talent who was in danger of burning out.

Successful implementation of any strategy requires making hard choices, trade-offs and resource allocation.

Phase 2: Ensure individuals prioritize their time in alignment with company priorities

With the completion of Phase 1, there will be visibility on the priorities as defined by top management at HQ. At the regional level down to the individual operating units, leaders will now have guidance on what they will focus on. This said, individuals will find the following tools useful. If Susan had taken reference from them, she would have utilized her time more effectively.

The Pareto Principle: Vilfredo Pareto (1848–1923) was an Italian engineer and economist. The Pareto Principle named after him states that 80% of consequences come from 20% of the causes, asserting an unequal relationship between inputs and outputs. On a macro scale, he noticed that 80% of the wealth in Italy was owned by 20% of the people. This concept of disproportion often holds true in many areas.

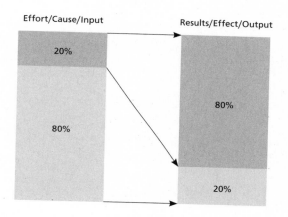

These are situations that we frequently encounter in real life:

- 20% of the time you expend will contribute to 80% of your key goals
- 20% of what you do may produce 80% of the impact you desire
- 20% of features in an app are used 80% of the time
- 20% of what you say will be remembered by 80% of the audience

Also known as the 80/20 rule or the Law of the Critical Few, it reminds us of the asymmetry between cause and effect. How exact are the values of 80 and 20? Not at all. We need not be fixated by the actual numbers. It could be 60/40, 70/30 or 90/10. All that matters is to pause and be selective before taking a slew of actions on multiple fronts. One or two well-placed activities may be all that is needed.

The Urgency vs Importance Matrix (Eisenhower Principle): Less is more. Dwight D. Eisenhower was the 34th President of the United States, from 1953 until 1961. He served as the Allied Forces Supreme

Commander during World War II. Those of us who have read about D-Day or watched the epic film *The Longest Day* will recall that Eisenhower launched the largest seaborne invasion in history of Nazi-occupied Western Europe. Its success was the major turning point in the war that led to the defeat of Nazi Germany.

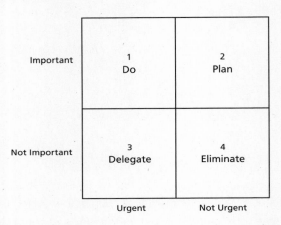

	Urgent	Not Urgent
Important	1 Do	2 Plan
Not Important	3 Delegate	4 Eliminate

The Urgency vs Importance Matrix encapsulates the thinking that facilitates deciding where to focus your time and resources each day. Prioritization is guided by the trade-off between urgency and importance. To get out of the time trap, it is important to be clear about the distinction between urgency and importance. A lot of people start the day by turning on the notebook computer and plunging into a flurry of activities that shout for their attention. Doing many things without asking why and when will lead to sheer waste of time.

Important activities are those that have passed the scrutiny of the Pareto Principle. Urgent activities are those that demand immediate attention because the consequences of not dealing with them are great. They are often outside our control, e.g. someone higher up wants something to be done now; an unexpected business opportunity suddenly presents itself; a flood of complaints is received about poor customer service; or something that you or your team did not foresee must be attended to now.

66

The four quadrants in the matrix are numbered 1 to 4. When urgency and importance coincide, it is priority 1 for the day. When something is important but not urgent, we have time to plan for it and get it done well. For instance, planning ahead for a new product launch in six months' time. Or preparing for a business presentation that will take place four weeks later. This will be priority 2, which means taking concrete actions within a certain timeframe. Letting this slip through procrastination is a common pitfall. This will feed into quadrant 1 and that's how people find themselves constantly fire-fighting. When you have items in quadrant 3, it is an opportunity to delegate them to some of your team members. But before doing this, have a chat with them on whether there is really a need to do that thing. People who work for you are busy too and it does not help to dump unimportant things on their lap. And finally, activities in quadrant 4 should be consciously taken off your list.

The To Do list: It is a great habit to start the day in a calm and relaxed state of mind. Identify the top 5 items that will go onto your To-Do list. The aim is to complete them by the end of the day. Usually this may require your personal attention. Some may need you to involve others such as your team members, peers and other stakeholders. It is useful to share your priorities with your teams. In some cases, let your bosses know as well so as to be aligned with them.

Review and reflect: Once again, less is more. In the course of your work day, it is a good practice to provide some *white space* in your calendar. These are short moments of about 15 minutes in between meetings or other activities to just pause, breathe deeply and gather your thoughts. Initially, blocking out blank spaces feels like an indulgence, but soon you will realize that it may be your single most important productivity tool.

Additionally, some people set aside 30 minutes before the start of the day. There are others who keep Friday afternoon for this purpose. If you have an executive assistant, discuss this with her so that she does not pack your day with endless activities.

Without this, you will drift from one meeting to another mindlessly. Some people have mentioned that at the end of a 12-hour day, they feel completely depleted. What was discussed and committed to early in the day becomes a distant memory.

At the end of the day, check your To Do list. What has been accomplished? What has gone well? What obstacles have you encountered? How can you improve further? What are key takeaways? What will be your next steps tomorrow? Next week?

Many people who have applied these simple methods have indeed found themselves managing their work day more productively. They break out of the vicious loop of endless activities feeding into each other.

8

BE WARY OF QUICK CONSENSUS

Why it's equally important to manage both agreement and disagreement

"If we are all in agreement on the decision – then I propose we postpone further discussion of this matter to give ourselves time to develop disagreement and perhaps gain some understanding of what the decision is all about."
Alfred P. Sloan,
Chairman of General Motors (1937–1956)

A few years ago, a global adhesives manufacturer, which I'll name Sarus, missed its earnings forecast for two consecutive quarters for the first time in its history. It had a sizeable presence in China, India, Japan, Korea and Southeast Asia. More agile competitors were nipping at their heels with innovative offerings, better technical support and lower prices.

When market forces were in their favor, the company had their hands full keeping up with insatiable demand from customers. The Asian operations were the star performer for the global business. To be sure, when they were on a hot streak, customer feedback had always been good but not great, as they would put it wryly. The GMs of the respective countries and functional heads were all focused on meeting their own KPIs. Their silo mentality translated into poor customer responsiveness and technical support. Suddenly there was consternation at HQ. Divestment of the business could happen unless they could turn it around quickly.

The president of APAC convened an offsite for all the top leaders.

Everyone present now knew that they had only one common goal: first to survive and then regain its competitive position. For that to happen, they would have to double down on collaboration. All the leaders were on board. But after the meeting, when they returned to their countries, friction and tension become manifest almost immediately.

No quick fixes

When businesses face strong headwinds, it becomes a wakeup call. Their leaders will emphasize their shared goals and the importance of working as one. But as people at Sarus discovered, the hoped-for collaboration may be elusive even after numerous meetings.

The problem is that leadership teams, like the organizations they lead, are not mechanistic entities but living organisms. If a machine is creaking, we can with some data and analysis determine the root cause(s) such as a worn-out bearing, and have it replaced. Then it should function smoothly again. Not so for a network of people who have different roles, priorities, self-interests and constituencies in the organization. Throw into the mix diverse personalities, perspectives and nationalities, all vying for recognition and scarce resources. And factor in the absence of mutual trust, interdependence and the spirit of give-and-take. Long-buried and unexamined issues such accountabilities, identities and power plays will now rise to the fore. As they gather pace and feed on each other, they will bedevil the organizational climate.

Four practices for collaboration

In my work with numerous leadership teams, I have witnessed the ebb and flow of emotions as members struggle with collaboration. The following diagram depicts four practices that will guide leaders in charting their journey towards collaboration.

1. Shared purpose: This is the cornerstone of collaboration. Leaders will invariably ask themselves many questions, silently and openly. What exactly is it that only through collaboration we can accomplish that we

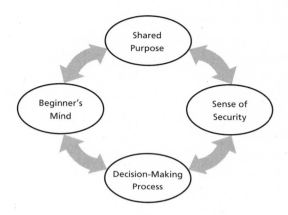

cannot otherwise? How will it impact the lives and work of people and the future of the organization? What is the value that I can bring to this undertaking? What do the other functions bring? All such questions need to be openly discussed so that everyone feels that their contributions will be consequential and compelling.

Consider the extraordinary rescue of 12 Thai boys and their young coach in June 2018. They were members of the Moo Pa ("Wild Boars" in Thai), a youth football team. After a routine practice they hiked into the Tham Luang cave system that snakes for 10 km beneath Thailand and Myanmar. A flash flood caught them off-guard. To escape, they went deeper into the caves and became marooned, with water rising rapidly.

News of their extreme peril captured the world's attention. Experts from all over the globe pitched in over the course of the 18-day ordeal. The final push involved a total of 90 divers – 40 from Thailand and 50 foreigners. What rallied a bunch of people, many of whom were total strangers, to collaborate so tirelessly and selflessly? It was a single-minded shared purpose: to get the 13 youths out alive and well. They succeeded. It was high-risk. Saman Gunan, a former Thai Navy Seal diver, paid with his life when he ran out of oxygen.

2. Sense of security: To work well as a team requires deep and candid discussions on all substantial matters. If people aren't speaking up, fear is in the workplace. It's a straight causal link between the sense of safety and people's ultimate commitment. If they can't disagree, then their agreement counts for nothing. This was what led to the conundrum that Sarus faced.

There are two aspects of sense of security. The first is psychological safety. This is the confidence in people to speak their minds and take risks because they know there will not be negative repercussions. The second aspect is linked to the threat of losing one's identity and standing when the territorial boundary marking out one's role is encroached on because of the messy nature of cross-group collaboration.

Sarus was losing out on new accounts because it was painfully slow in responding to bids. Before a bid submission, Finance had to complete a credit risk analysis for new cases. This process could be speeded up if Sales and Finance collaborated. Someone in Sales then suggested that response time could even become market-beating if Finance could teach them to assess and structure risk.

Here was an idea worthy of serious consideration. But Finance wasn't ready for it. By equipping Sales to do risk analysis on their own, wouldn't it be asking the fox to guard the henhouse? If credit risk analysis, a highly valued expertise went to Sales, would Finance now have a lesser role? It represented an existential threat.

3. Decision-making process: The time will come when the leadership team has to make critical strategic decisions. It is not going to be easy. Leadership teams are legislatures, if you will. Each member, with the exception of the most senior leader, represents their own constituency, from Sales to Marketing, Engineering, HR, R&D, Finance, Legal and Supply Chain. Despite having agreed to take off their functional hats and act in the larger interest of the company, there will still be turf interests to protect.

The three most popular approaches are: (1) Ask the parties with differing views to present their cases so that other members can weigh in from their supposedly impartial standpoints; (2) Take a vote to seek a majority view; and (3) Let the boss decide. Of these three methods, the first is fraught with tension, and will likely to lead to dissatisfaction with the outcome. However, if managed wisely, it can become a competitive advantage because new and creative ideas are unleashed. I'll discuss this in greater detail presently. The second and third are overused default options because people want to avoid heated arguments, taking sides and making hard choices. This is a cop-out and will haunt the organization to no end.

Most leaders at the pinnacle of a company are individual high performers with egos to match. When it comes down to pitching for their preferred solutions, the natural instinct is to advocate theirs as the best course of action. Winning endorsement is the only objective. In such an emotional state, differing views and questions are to be defended vigorously against. This is the default mode of communication in most companies. The precious opportunity of tapping into the collective wisdom of other people is forfeited!

A more helpful approach is to foster a dialogue that balances advocacy with inquiry. While articulating your own views, be genuinely interested to hear the opinions and thoughts of your colleagues. Imagine how the mood will lighten up if leaders say with humility and sincerity, "I have an idea to share and will really value your inputs as I may be missing something."

Most cultures, especially in Asia and the Middle-East, are uncomfortable with expressing conflicting and divergent views. It is the desire to preserve harmony and not cause loss of face. We can make a paradigm shift if we depersonalize and depoliticize conflict. Start by setting the ground rules. Define what are useful and not useful behaviors. Then introduce a process by which members play different roles such a proposer, a devil's advocate, a supporter, a bystander and a moderator. Over the course of months, by adopting this decision-making process, members will have the opportunity to play, and become adept with, all these roles.

To paraphrase the ancient Chinese sages, "Be grateful to people who support you. Be very grateful to people who oppose you." By honing our skills in this new mode of dialogue, ego is given a rest. Everyone eagerly participates in the learning journey.

4. The beginner's mind: Heads of businesses or functions often see themselves as experts in their disciplines. Their deep knowledge is of great value when addressing challenges. But deep expertise and experience can leave leaders incurious, blinkered and vulnerable – even in their own fields. This is the expertise trap. There are many examples of once great icons who have fallen because of this. Motorola executives in the 1990s became so obsessed with the Six Sigma continuous improvement methodology, which they had pioneered and developed, that they missed the significance of the industry's shift to digital technology and fell far behind their competitors. Others include Nokia, Kodak and BlackBerry.

Shunryu Suzuki, a Zen monk, has taught the practice of the *beginner's mind* to avoid the expertise trap.

> *"In the beginner's mind there are many possibilities,*
> *but in the expert's mind there are few."*
> Shunryu Suzuki, Zen Buddhist Master

When leaders are faced with the pressure of picking critical choices for their companies, it is useful to take a pause. Listen up. Welcome questions. Sometimes, a single question can change everything.

The journey towards consensus matters far more than the consensus itself

Many leadership teams mistakenly believe that to kick-start collaboration, they should identify their common goal and then execute relentlessly. This can open up a can of worms instead. It is more productive to view collaboration as a journey involving four key practices. When at last they arrive at a consensus, it will be one that all feel they are a part of and have ownership to turn into success.

9

THE HIGH-PERFORMING LEADERSHIP TEAM

Understanding what it takes to build great teams

"Good teams become great when members trust each other enough to surrender the Me for the We."
Phil Jackson, Basketball Hall of Famer

The value of a high-performing team has long been recognized. As Covid-19 and digital technology reshape the notion of the workplace and how work is done, teamwork is becoming even more critical as remote working becomes the norm, virtual collaboration more commonplace, and cross-cultural partnership more necessary. Teams instead of individuals have become the fundamental operating unit. In countless studies involving C-suite executives representing a diverse range of businesses and sizes, an unequivocal finding is: efficient ongoing collaboration has a profound impact on business innovation, performance, culture and the bottom line.

Is this anything new? In the past few decades even in Western societies that prize individualism over collective action, there has been an obsession with teams. And in Eastern cultures which value putting the collective good ahead of individuals' goals, teamwork has always been the preferred mode for working in organizations. The received wisdom is that teamwork unleashes greater creativity and productivity.

How much of such expectations has been borne out by reality at the workplace? In my consultancy work with teams, I usually begin by asking leaders to respond privately to this question: When people work together on cross-functional projects, will the job probably (a) get done faster, (b) take longer to finish, or (c) not get done? Those who have little experience with teams will choose (a). Most who work in teams extensively know better. It is either (b) or even (c).

While the possibility exists that a high-performing team can indeed evoke extraordinary results, research has shown that teams generally underperform despite the extra resources they have. And when the stakes get higher with senior executive teams, the impact can be catastrophic. The dysfunctional ones can slow down, derail, or even paralyze the whole company. There is a mutually reinforcing relationship between senior leadership team effectiveness and the company's culture.

What is a team?

It is quite common to hear colleagues being labelled a team even though they've just been hurriedly summoned for a briefing on different pieces of work that each needs to carry out on their own. And in all likelihood, they may not come together again. This is a work group rather than a team. So what is a team? At the most fundamental, let's start by distinguishing between them.

- **Work groups** are characterized by the independent nature of the work that each person performs. It is quite minimal in terms of interaction and interdependence. When each person has done their part, all they need to do is to report to the person who oversees the overall work.

- **Teams** on the other hand require members to interact and collaborate with each other. The nature of their work is highly interdependent. Nobody can work in silos as what each does will impact the work of other members.

Conditions for leadership team effectiveness

The basics of team effectiveness were identified Richard Hackman, Ruth Wageman and two other colleagues in their book entitled *Senior Leadership Teams*. Drawing upon their study of 120 top teams from around the world, they stipulated six conditions as follows:

1. **Real team:** To work well together, team members need to know who actually are on the team. These people share responsibility and accountability for the collective outcome. There are others whom they may call upon for counsel and help but they are not team members. Team membership needs to be relatively stable but can change according to circumstances. Teams can include members who are culturally diverse, geographically dispersed and virtual.

2. **Compelling direction:** This is the cornerstone of all great teams. It defines the shared purpose for their existence as a team. It must be consequential and challenging. What exactly is it that through collaboration they must accomplish that they otherwise cannot? How will it impact the lives and work of people and the future of the enterprise? These lead to a sense of shared identity and context.

3. **The right people:** Team composition needs to be of the right balance of competencies. A healthy blend of technical and social skills, as well as diversity in age, gender and race can engender a more creative working climate. Ensuring the right people are in the team is hugely important. Team leaders who select the wrong people or postpone the inevitable decision to remove misfits will witness the descent of their teams into endless bouts of infighting and recrimination. It is also better to have a team size as small as possible to avoid what psychologists call social loafing. Economists call the same thing free-riding.

4. **Solid team structure:** Effective team dynamics requires well-defined work and social processes. Too prescriptive a structure leads to a robotic environment devoid of humanism and fresh ideas. Having a laissez-faire setup can be just as debilitating, resulting in a gridlock and dysfunctional behaviors. Defining and agreeing on norms of conduct is thus vital. The right norms can energize interaction and raise a team's collective intelligence. In such a setting, members are socially sensitive, respect each other's views and will ensure that everyone has an equal chance to express themselves, e.g. conversational turn-taking.

   Being clear about what it means to work as a team requires deep discussions upfront. Not every matter requires everyone to be involved. Certain things can best be done by one person or a sub-group. There will be matters and times when everyone needs to be collaborating. But in other instances, members willingly rely on others' expertise, judgment and experience, thereby demonstrating interdependence. And there needs to be well-defined processes for effective meetings, timely conflict resolution and decision-making that transcend narrow functional interests.

5. **Supportive context:** For a work team to thrive, a supportive organization context is a prerequisite. This includes a company culture that values collaboration, a recognition and reward system that reinforces good team performance, access to data and information, an educational system that offers training, and the availability of material resources required for the job.

6. **Team coaching:** The best teams are continually being coached and are coaching themselves to evolve, learn and grow. Feedback and regular reviews are important tools that will help raise awareness and enable everyone to step up to a higher level. While having a strong team leader is critical, team leadership is not solely the responsibility of the team leader. A good team will

develop the habit of pausing regularly to look at what has transpired and to provide candid inputs to each other. Their members speak to each other frequently and casually to coach each other in and out of meetings.

The team development journey

Team leaders may leverage these six conditions as a recipe for building their teams either from scratch or even with inherited teams. The team development journey may roughly be broken into the following phases:

1. Team design and formation
2. Team launch
3. Evaluation of effectiveness
4. Team coaching
5. Ongoing monitoring of effectiveness
6. Sustaining and renewal

The high-performance leadership team framework

If you have a team that has been working together for a few months, performing a team effectiveness diagnostic can provide data and insights about how the team is performing. There are numerous surveys that provide such a baseline. The High-Performance Leadership Team Framework that I have developed and used extensively with clients globally is one such diagnostic. It is an online survey that all team members, including the leader, will complete. It consists of eight dimensions:

1. **Shared purpose:** This is the undisputed key determinant of collaboration. It serves as a bridge between what the members are doing and the overall organizational purpose. In each one of us, there is a primal need to connect what we do with giving back to the community. Hence, if we work for a construction company that seeks to provide quality and affordable housing, our shared purpose as a cross-functional team may be to "simplify

processes to reduce cost of construction and improve quality to bring affordable housing to the community."

2. **Interdependence:** In order to achieve synergy, team members will need to recognize and appreciate that members bring with them unique experience, expertise and talent. By leveraging this range of abilities, the net outcome will be more than the sum of their individual capabilities: $1+1>2$. When working independently, members may trip over each other, resulting in $1+1<2$.

3. **Boundary spanning:** Members actively reach out beyond functions, business boundaries and geography to seek fresh insights, emerging trends and formulate new perspectives. This is a practice to ensure that the team is constantly vigilant about what goes on in the external environment.

4. **Collective accountability:** Members feel accountable for each other's performance, well-being and learning. This is why teams

are formed. When members buy into a shared purpose, they will do what it takes to help others succeed. It is a given that members will need to be individually competent and able to do what is required.

5. **Ways of working:** There are effective processes for conducting meetings, decision-making and resolving conflicts. By spending time to define and agree on these three processes, they ensure that they have a well-oiled system to facilitate their interactions. Without this, teams will spin their wheels endlessly.

6. **Review, feedback and development:** The team review their effectiveness regularly, seek feedback from each other, practice peer coaching and have a development plan for ongoing development.

7. **Team leadership:** Members feel confident of, and are inspired by, the leadership that is provided by the team leader and collectively by each other. As teams evolve, members take it upon themselves to define the directions that they should be pursuing. They do not leave it to the official leader. And the leader creates space for the members to step up.

8. **Psychological safety:** There is a safe and nurturing team culture so that everybody will openly voice their opinions without fear of repercussion. This is such an important factor that I'll discuss it separately in Chapter 11.

The diagnostic report

The diagnostic report consists of quantitative ratings of the items pertaining to the eight factors. It also has a section in which members will provide comments to open-ended questions. Such a report is a treasure trove of information. Members will benefit most when they discuss and examine lowest- and highest-scored effectiveness ratings. They will also find it illuminating to compare ratings and comments provided by the leader and the team members. A well-facilitated intervention will lead to discovery of blind spots and the proverbial elephant in the room. The most useful outcome will be the identification of critical issues and opportunities. A concise team action plan as well as a short list of individual actions will define the way forward for all in the team.

For ongoing monitoring, it is recommended that a temperature check be done at six-monthly intervals using a simplified version of the diagnostic. Displaying the pre-and post-survey results in a spider diagram is a visually powerful way to show progress.

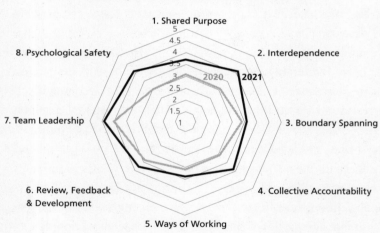

Leadership Team Effectiveness, 2020 vs 2021

Is your team really making a difference?

How does one know how much more effective a team has become? There are three criteria: (1) collective output that meets or exceeds customers' and stakeholders' expectations, (2) collaborative ability, and (3) individual members' learning. The higher scores in the spider diagram must lead to observable and measurable improvements in these three criteria. Let's consider each of these criteria in turn.

Collective output: The diagnostic survey will solicit the inputs from stakeholders such as internal customers, peers, business partners and the people in the company. All these constituencies will tell you how you are performing. The employee engagement survey is a sure way of finding out whether your people think you have made a positive impact on them.

Collaborative ability: How well a leadership team work with each other is highly visible. People are constantly observing them and being impacted by their interactions and actions. It has a contagious effect on the company culture. Members of leadership teams frequently struggle with deciding which team is their first priority. Is it the leadership team they are part of? Or the functional teams that they lead?

Without a doubt, Team Number One is the Leadership Team. This is because the leadership team define the priorities and set the directions for the rest of the company. By devoting the required time and effort to bring out the best in the leadership team, members do themselves and the company a great service. With this, they can provide their functional teams clear directions and guidance, secure in the knowledge that these have all been agreed above. In turn, functional teams proceed confidently to work with their cross-functional peers, knowing that there has been alignment at the top.

But if on the other hand, leadership team members misguidedly treat their own functional teams as top priority, then the leadership team sessions will degenerate into a United Nations-like forum. Countries come with their own agendas and battle with each other to get what they desire for their countries. The net outcome: big powerful nations dominate. Small countries are marginalized. Lots of talk and emotions but no collective progress.

Individual members' learning: The dynamics of a great team leads to a virtuous cycle in all members' development because they provide feedback and coaching to each other. This is the concept of co-elevation: taking responsibility for your teammates' success as you do your own.

Again, over time, the difference is powerfully visible to the members themselves and people around them.

While building high-performing senior leadership teams is fraught with challenges and difficulties, no company can afford not to unleash the power and magic of collaboration. Today's demands for more effective teamwork will become more pressing and complex than in the past. By adopting a systematic approach to designing and developing your teams, your chances of success will be greatly enhanced.

10

WHY WE NEED TO UNLEARN

Obsolete ideas must make way for better ones

*"To attain knowledge, acquire something every day.
To be wise, drop something every day."*
Laozi

Each year during summer, there are massive firestorms across California. Many firefighters lose their lives trying to bring the blazes under control. Real-life cases are legion about courageous firefighters who are trapped in exploding fires and have to battle their way out. There have been tragedies reported in which firefighters perished a short distance from safety. As the safety zone was within sight, the most sensible action would be to drop their heavy equipment and run for their lives. Yet, many of them refused to do so, were engulfed by fire, and died with their tools beside them. It was reported that one firefighter perished with his backpack on and a chainsaw in his hand, a mere 250 feet from safety.

These aren't isolated incidents. There are many other examples such as air force fighter pilots who refused to eject from their distressed aircraft, and died as a result. In 2014, the South Korean ferry *Sewol* was en route from Inchon to Jeju with hundreds of children and teachers for a school excursion. The ferry was visibly overloaded and structurally unsound. Nobody, the captain and his crew no less, felt anything was amiss. Along the journey, the vessel made a sudden turn and started to list dangerously. Orders were passed down for all to remain in their cabins. Most people, including the vice-principal and teachers, obeyed unquestioningly. More than 300 passengers, mostly children, were drowned. There were a few survivors though. These were some children who took matters into their own hands. They defied their elders, clambered onto the upper deck and jumped overboard.

Prisoners of our thoughts

What is the common thread that runs across the anecdotes that resulted in the tragic ends of the firefighters, the air force fighter pilots and the 300 passengers on *Sewol*? They were all trapped by the years of training and conditioning that they had undergone. Fire suppression, like almost any kind of profession, calls for capabilities involving tools and knowledge. Skillful use of tools is the mark of a seasoned firefighter and central to that person's identity. No self-respecting firefighters would drop their tools even under conditions of danger. Similarly for the fighter pilots. The passengers on *Sewol* had all been raised under the Korean culture and school education which places a premium on obedience and respect for authority. Everybody submitted to orders, except a handful.

The incidents are analogies of a larger aspect of the human condition. When we have assimilated concepts, habits and assumptions that we have found useful, we tend to hold onto them steadfastly. This is so even in the face of changing environmental conditions. The latter occurs because we frequently fail to notice and acknowledge what is happening outside us. It may even be the case of willful blindness. Such could be the case with the failure of the captain and his crew to raise the alarm over the visible signs that the *Sewol* was not seaworthy. In other words, people become prisoners of their own thoughts.

What is unlearning?

There is a well-known story, probably apocryphal, about a self-confident leader who traveled a great distance to seek enlightenment from a wise Zen master. A few minutes into their conversation, it became obvious that the leader was full of his own opinions and knowledge. He interrupted the master repeatedly with his own stories. The monk calmly suggested that they should have tea. As the master poured his guest a cup, it soon became full. Yet, he kept pouring until the cup overflowed and the tea ran onto the table and onto the floor. The visitor cried "Stop! The cup is full already. Can't you see?" The master replied with a smile. "You are like this cup — so full of ideas that nothing more will fit in. Come back to me with an empty mind."

Although we all possess immense capacity to learn new things, what we have accepted as truths will pose a big obstacle to acquiring a new perspective. It is the "stickiness" factor. As we have seen in the earlier examples, old and obsolete ideas can shut out new and better ideas. If we think we already know, it is difficult to be open to new knowledge, especially that which contradicts what we know.

Why we need to unlearn

Here are the key reasons:

- **The rapid obsolescence of knowledge.** Take a glance at one of your own textbooks. Even if you are a recent graduate, you will find that the version that you studied is quite outdated. You shouldn't be surprised: facts are changing around us all the time. Whether it's what we were told to be the truth – the population of the planet; the fastest time for the 100 meter dash; drinking red wine is good for your health; abstaining from dairy products, tai chi, yoga and acupuncture have unproven medical benefits – knowledge is in constant flux. If we stick with what we have been taught, it will be akin to trying to explore a country you are visiting with an obsolete map.

- **The world is changing so rapidly.** A recent report authored by the Institute for the Future and a panel of 20 tech, business and academic experts from around the world mentions that the pace of change will get a lot faster. People will need to learn "in the moment" using new technologies such as augmented reality and virtual reality. The ability to gain new knowledge will be more valuable than the knowledge itself.

- **The workforce of the future is already here.** Millennials and the younger Gen Z will inspire meaningful ideas that will reshape the future of work. There are four major shifts that can be anticipated. They include a growing emphasis on self-development, remote working, freelance roles and future-proofing strategies. The latter means that younger workers take it upon themselves to continually upgrade and learn new skills so they can remain employable in the decades ahead. If they are not getting what they want from their employers, they will seek development opportunities elsewhere.

> *"In times of change, learners inherit the earth,*
> *while the learned find themselves beautifully equipped*
> *to deal with a world that no longer exists."*
> Eric Hoffer,
> American moral and social philosopher

How Microsoft unlearned and reinvented itself

More than ten years ago, Microsoft dominated the tech industry. It was the wealthiest corporation in the world. But since 2000, as Apple, Google and Facebook whizzed by, it fell flat in every arena it entered: e-books, music, search, social networking and mobile phones.

Microsoft co-founder and first CEO Bill Gates confessed that his mismanagement of Microsoft's mobile effort was his greatest mistake. Microsoft missed out on the mega-buck market by letting Google turn Android into the only real alternative to Apple's iPhone. Company insiders reveal that loyalty and obsession with Windows and the Office suite of productivity software prevented Microsoft from recognizing and adopting emerging technologies. According to a former Microsoft exec-utive, "Windows was the god – everything had to work with Windows." Ideas about mobile computing with a user experience that was cleaner than with a Windows PC were deemed unimportant and killed off. Microsoft's second CEO Steve Ballmer famously laughed at the iPhone, calling it the "most expensive phone in the world and it doesn't appeal to business customers because it doesn't have a keyboard." He was com-pletely blindsided by the touch-friendly era Apple was ushering in. This was NIH (Not Invented Here) thinking at the very top. And it shows how thousands of smart people can be held captive by the mindset of their top leaders.

In February 2014, 22-year veteran Satya Nadella replaced Ballmer as the third CEO. By then, the company had been viewed as spiraling towards obsolescence. The unbridled power of the Windows and Office divisions to dictate the direction of product development was only one of the myriad problems unfolding within Microsoft that served to crush innovation. There were far larger issues: bloated bureaucracy, brutal cor-porate politics and infighting, fear and insecurity in the workforce, and top executives completely out of touch with the needs of a new genera-tion of users fascinated by the networked economy.

Nadella knew that the company had to unlearn and relearn. He was determined to make Microsoft a company where "smart, curious, ambitious people" could do "their best work." The single overarch-ing metaphor that he adopted to guide the transformation was Carol Dweck's concept of the growth mindset. This contrasted with the fixed mindset that pervaded Microsoft in its so-called lost decade (see box on growth vs fixed mindsets).

Nadella set about building a new senior team comprising people who were willing to raise tough issues and commit to collaboration once decisions were reached. He chose people who were results-oriented and also respectful and empathetic to employees at all levels. Nadella urged leaders to model the growth mindset, and he played role-model-in-chief in this regard. Funding to Windows was cut, and an enormous cloud

Growth mindset vs fixed mindset

Carol Dweck of Stanford University found in her research that individuals can be placed on a continuum according to their implicit view of where ability comes from. Some believe their success is based on innate ability; these are said to have a fixed mindset. Others, who believe their success is based on hard work, learning, training and doggedness, are said to have a growth mindset.

The power of our beliefs has a major impact on the course of our lives. These may be beliefs we're aware or unaware of, but they strongly affect what we want and whether we succeed in getting them. There is a famous saying that exemplifies this: "Whether you think you can, or you think you can't – you're right."

A growth mindset is the belief that abilities and understanding can be developed. People with the growth mindset are convinced that they can get smarter, more intelligent, and more talented through putting in time and effort. A fixed mindset assumes that our character, intelligence and creative ability are carved in stone, which we can't change in any meaningful way. Success is the affirmation of these qualities. Those with a fixed mindset may believe that intelligence cannot be enhanced, or that you either "have it or you don't" when it comes to abilities and talents.

This difference in mindset may lead to marked differences in behavior as well. If someone believes intelligence and abilities are immutable traits, they are not likely to put in much effort to change their inherent intelligence and abilities. Why try to effect changes that are beyond your control? Even more insidiously, they may adopt a defensive attitude towards learning new things or undertaking a challenging assignment. You may have met some accomplished people who are reluctant to stretch themselves further. A fixed mindset convinces them that it is better to play "not to lose" than to "play to win."

On the other hand, those who embrace the growth mindset believe that their initial talents, aptitudes or temperament can change and grow through application and effort. They are therefore very willing to put in extra time and effort to achieve more ambitious goals. The passion for stretching yourself and sticking to it even (and especially) when it's not going well, is the hallmark of the growth mindset. This enables people to thrive during the some of the most challenging times in their lives.

computing business was built. Within five years, Microsoft reinvented itself. It has now taken its place as one of the world's most valuable tech companies alongside Amazon, Apple and Google's Alphabet Inc.

> *"Just because some people can do something with little*
> *or no training, it doesn't mean that others can't do it*
> *(and sometimes do it even better) with training."*
> Carol Dweck, Professor of Psychology,
> Stanford University

How can leaders learn to unlearn?

The biggest obstacle to unlearning is that we aren't aware of our assumptions. Our assumptions are the lens through which we see and interpret what appears before us. For instance, if we habitually drive to work using a certain preferred route, after many years we no longer think about it. We assume that it is the best commute. One day, we happen to take a cab to work. The cabbie takes a different route and it turns out to be less congested and gets us to the office much earlier. Now we wish we had discovered this different commute years back.

Using this as an example, the way to unlearn and relearn may take the following steps:

1. **Adopt an inquisitive mindset:** What are certain ways of doing things that either originate from you or have always been done that you now start to question? You may have heard comments from others that people are facing issues with these processes. Or it is a strange nagging feeling inside you. Find out more. Be curious. Read up and expose yourself to different sources of ideas. Ask for the advice of people who are impacted by the processes. I would add further that you might be reluctant to change the practice, especially if it had been championed by you. You might even have taken umbrage in the past at suggestions that some

changes could be profitably pursued. Approached with some humility, these are clear signs that this is the process to focus on.

2. **Experiment:** Select a new idea that appeals to you. Test it out and observe the impact on yourself and others. Involve others in your experiment. This first experiment may lead to many more that others may likewise initiate. Reflect and ask yourself what you have learned. Share your learning with others. Are there other opportunities to exploit now?

3. **Embrace failure as a learning opportunity:** Every experiment that you and your colleagues make will lead to new learning and discovery, even if it does not succeed the first time. When an organization embraces the growth mindset, it will acquire learning agility, a key prerequisite for success.

11

PSYCHOLOGICAL SAFETY

Fostering a climate for rich conversation and learning

"When I can't disagree, then my agreement
means nothing."
A young and thoughtful leader

To build high-performing teams, there are eight dimensions that were described in Chapter 9. Of these, psychological safety is probably the most fundamental. Amy Edmondson, professor at Harvard Business School, first identified the concept of psychological safety in work teams in 1999. Since then, the concept has gained wide acceptance across all organizations and industries seeking to be more inclusive and raise employee engagement. In teamwork it is a sine qua non. In a 2015 study on teamwork by Google, they identified five keys to a successful Google team. Four of these involve dependability, clarity, meaning and impact. And the single most important variable? Psychological safety.

Why are people afraid of speaking up?

Let's start with three vignettes which will be quite familiar.

Consider what happens in a department meeting chaired by a senior manager. You are one of the eight attendees. One key item is to make a decision on an important project. Two of your peers, Vicci and Amit have diametrically opposing views on which way to go. They have never seen eye-to-eye with each other over the years. And it is gearing up to be a competition between them. The debate is getting quite heated. Everybody knows that the boss favors Vicci's approach. While her ideas are sound, they would be even more practical if she adopted some of Amit's. Based on past experience, you know that the boss does not take kindly to being second-guessed. He is known to have a short fuse. Should you or should you not chime in?

Another situation that you may face is an initiative that the company wants to roll out such as a new rewards and compensation scheme. The HR head is explaining the details in a global video call. Ahead of this, everybody knows through the grapevine that it is a fait accompli. There are quite a few things that don't sound right. Privately many colleagues have expressed their concerns. Today, no one is saying anything though. Will you take the risk to speak up?

Finally, consider the 360-degree feedback exercise that companies conduct to solicit feedback from all levels about leaders' performance. It is done online and respondents are assured of anonymity. In quite a few organizations though, employees don't trust the system: they have evidence that there is traceability to persons who have provided the feedback. And retribution from bosses can be swift and career-limiting. Therefore employees go along with the charade. They couch their words and put a positive spin to all their remarks.

In the three vignettes, the behaviors are representative of how thousands, even millions, will react in similar situations around the world. The underlying factor is self-preservation. Employees choose to keep their opinions to themselves when they sense that speaking up will put them in harm's way.

> *"Psychological safety is a belief that one will not*
> *be punished or humiliated for speaking up with*
> *ideas, questions, concerns or mistakes."*
> Amy Edmondson, Harvard Business School

Most workplaces don't meet this standard, and their performance suffers. A 2018 Gallup poll found that only three in ten US employees strongly agree with the statement that their opinions matter at work. Gallup calculated that by moving this ratio to six in ten employees, there would be a 27% reduction in turnover, 40% reduction in safety incidents, and a 12% increase in productivity. The consequences of this conspiracy of silence can be devastating.

The first cases of Covid-19 were detected in Wuhan city in late December 2019. Dr. Li Wenliang, the whistleblower who warned about the virus on social media, was quickly reprimanded on December 30. He later died due to the infection. By silencing Dr. Li, Chinese and international experts missed the critical opportunities to prevent a global pandemic.

Another infamous incident, still fresh in the mind of many people, is Volkswagen's diesel emissions scandal in 2015. The company had sanctioned the installation of a software designed to falsify emissions-testing results. This directive came from the highest echelons of management no less. Many people in the company knew what was going on, but did not raise the flag. As VW learned the hard way, failure to create a speak-up culture poses risks that go far beyond financial calamity.

Building psychological safety

Psychological safety does not mean that the environment is stress-free and people are so kind and caring that "anything goes." It is not about making people "comfortable," not adhering to high standards or letting some slack while others slog. The diagram on the next page discusses the tensions to be balanced between psychological safety and accountability.

Leaders have two major tasks. First, they must create a climate that spurs learning and receptivity to new ideas and thinking. Second, they must set high standards to inspire and enable people to reach them. One lever without the countervailing influence of the other will be ineffective. Absent both, people descend into the apathy zone: indifference compounded by awareness that nobody cares. When psychological safety is high and there is no accountability, it becomes a comfort zone with a lot of talk and no real effort. If leaders set high performance standards but do not create psychological safety, people are driven into the anxiety zone: fear, helplessness, resentment and frustration.

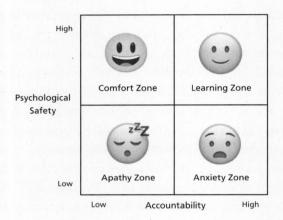

The aim is to enable all to operate in the learning zone. This is where employees feel empowered to voice their opinions because they know they matter, and there will not be retribution. At the same time, they have a sense of ownership to turn into reality the ideas that they have helped co-create.

The leader's tool kit for building psychological safety

Creating psychological safety in a company requires a major cultural makeover. It is not as easy as installing an app, so to speak. Or sending the employees to a one-day training program while the higher echelons stay ensconced at HQ. It takes a systemic effort starting from the top, role-modeling the new behavioral norms and walking the talk, again and again.

Leaders may consider adopting three steps:

1. Set the stage. Break the traditional habit of rushing to solutions. When things are cut and dried, people know what to do. However, when faced with uncertain and complex issues, there is no clear path ahead. This is when leaders need the collective inputs from everybody. Frame the work as a learning opportunity, not an execution problem. Start by saying that the issue can best be addressed if everybody participates actively. It is not time for execution yet, so let's pause and tap into the collective and diverse ideas of all of us. Ask questions, create space for deeper conversations and reflection. Although it seems a little contrived, if a few well-regarded colleagues at different levels can role-play this in a spontaneous way, it will bring greater clarity to others.

2. Acknowledge your own fallibility. There is no more powerful way for the senior leaders to signal their own willingness to learn than to admit that they are committed to continuous learning. The concept of unlearning is a great practice to inculcate. As Microsoft CEO Nadella puts it, shift from a Know-It-All to Learn-It-All. This is not easy. In many companies, leaders have a need to project an air of knowing everything. It takes courage and willingness to be vulnerable to sincerely tell them that you need their help.

Demonstrating humility also includes acknowledging your own blind spots and shortcomings. Everyone has these, no matter how high up the organization they are. By sharing this appropriately, employees see leaders as humans just like they themselves: wanting to do their best, but not always equipped with the skills, and wisdom, to do so. This will go down really well in most of the Western cultures in which there is a greater measure of egalitarianism. In the cultures in the East, there is expectation that leaders need to be confident and be in the know. Although the digital economy has upended this notion of the all-knowing leader, I recommend approaching this gradually. The older generation of employees will be rather ambivalent. But I expect that with time, they, the Millennials and Gen Z, will warm up and appreciate the wisdom of humility in their leaders.

3. Demonstrate support for risk-taking. It is imperative that leaders at all levels respond positively to the risks that people take. This can be manifested in various forms. Expression of support and appreciation is one. Encouraging new ideas and providing resources to test them out is another. With risks, there will inevitably be setbacks and failures. Leaders need to collectively get their heads around this challenge. An approach to adopt is to create a *safe-to-fail* environment to encourage employees to try out new approaches.

One CEO I know encourages his senior leaders to host monthly one-hour sessions to share about failures that have occurred and what they have learned from them. Some years ago, the Chief Scientific Officer at Eli Lilly introduced "failure parties" to honor intelligent, high-quality scientific experiments that failed to achieve desired results. By destigmatizing failures, a psychologically safe environment is built for thoughtful risks. When people show up, they all learn about the key takeaways from these experiments. This enhances the chances of success in future experiments in the rest of the company.

Creating a climate of psychological safety is not easy. But the investment is well worth it. Only when people feel psychologically safe will they speak up to offer new ideas.

12

DOING LESS, ACHIEVING MORE

Discover the concept of effortless effort

"The Dao never does anything,
yet through it everything is done.
If those in power observe this,
the world will develop naturally."
Laozi

One of Laozi's key teachings is the concept of *wei wu wei*, which literally means doing non-doing. This is a recognition of the natural, universal force known as the Dao. The Dao flows without effort and, like water, goes where it will, effecting change and growth. Excessive human strivings cannot contribute to good behavior, inner peace, or empathy with others because they are not in tune with nature. Haven't we tried very hard in pursuit of some objectives only to realize later that we could have adopted a simpler way? Perhaps with no intervention on our part?

A fitting metaphor of this paradox presented itself recently. I had completed an errand at a supermarket and was heading towards a car-park. A few lots away, a man was reverse-parking his car. He succeeded at his first attempt. But the woman seated next to him came out, apparently not quite satisfied, as she felt the car was parked too much to the left. Then began a series of iterations to get the car parked "properly." It took all of three minutes as the driver did as instructed. I watched the goings-on with great interest. The driver wore a pained look throughout.

Finally, when the woman was satisfied, the car was parked no differently than the first time.

Laozi is not an apologist for loafing or sloth. He does not advocate hiding in a cave to dissociate ourselves from the cares of the world. We may not understand his teachings at first because they seem counter-intuitive to our modern way of thinking. Laozi teases us patiently as he reminds us that we are but transient inhabitants on planet Earth. Millions before us have left without a trace when their time was up. So will we. So will the generations to come. Nature has been around for eons and will continue forever. She has her own rhythm. She has her own clock. She orchestrates billions of activities with grace and no hurry.

To be sure, worthwhile achievements do not drop onto one's lap from the sky. They require clear thinking, talent and persistence. But doing too much and moving too fast is counterproductive and even detrimental. This is the quiet and consistent message that Mother Nature has been trying to teach us. We lead more fulfilling lives when we work in harmony with nature. She is offering us an alternative perspective to the habit of over-managing our affairs.

"Take time for all great things:
great haste makes great waste."
Benjamin Franklin

How an over-zealous manager learns to trust his teams

Susanto is a leader at an American consumer products company. Two years ago, when his boss Hans repatriated back to Germany, Susanto was tapped as the next supply chain director. Among myriad responsibilities, Susanto oversees two plants which manufacture products for the retail operations in various parts of the world. Susanto is located in Jakarta while the two factories are in Thailand and Vietnam.

He is as driven and hands-on a manager as you can find. For the last two years, he has split his time three ways between Jakarta, Thailand and Vietnam. The work and travel schedule is punishing. He seems to be working 24/7. His predecessor Hans had a more relaxed approach as he used Jakarta as his base and delegated the responsibilities for the manufacturing operations to leaders in Thailand and Vietnam. But then, as Susanto rationalizes, Hans was an old hand in the job.

The stress is building up rapidly. One Sunday, Susanto collapses when walking his dog. He is overcome with exhaustion, lack of sleep and dehydration. But as he has a robust constitution, he is up and running after a week's rest. Then the Covid-19 pandemic arrives. Due to the lockdown, travel between countries ceases abruptly. He worries incessantly about what will happen in the plants. For eight months he works out of Jakarta, communicating via video calls with the leaders in both plants. As the months wear on, he notices to his disbelief that both plants are humming, even exceeding the global standards set for all plants around the world. The leadership teams have come into their own. The plant managers have stepped out of the shadow cast by Susanto. On Susanto's part, he has discovered that his people grow and become more independent when he leads less.

Why doing too much may be counterproductive

Here the key reasons why addiction to action may be self-defeating:

- **It may damage your well-being.** The human body follows a circadian rhythm that governs our sleep-wake cycle. When Susanto disrupts it chronically in his 24/7 back-breaking routine, he jeopardizes his health. Like an achievement-seeking missile, he starts and ends his day with only one thing in mind: he must be with his people. They can't do without his guidance. This is an illusion, as he has found out.

- **Stifles other people's growth:** Too much guidance is as stifling as being completely indifferent to your team's developmental needs. By doing a little less, you can create some space for them to explore new ideas and pathways for themselves.

- **Sometimes you just don't know:** There will be times when you just don't know what's best. Leaders aren't expected to have all the answers. It's simply not possible. Why then make a pretense of knowing everything? Acknowledging it and letting others participate in co-creating solutions can be liberating and empowering.

- **Going with the flow:** This is the central theme of Laozi's teaching. Sense the natural rhythm in the activities around you; go with the flow. If you've ever experienced a time when you excelled in what you were doing and lost all sense of time, you were in the state of flow. A good athlete achieves flow when the right move happens by itself, effortlessly, without any conscious effort. The game plays itself, the painting paints itself. We can't tell the dancer from the dance. It only happens because the dancer has learned to trust the superior intelligence of her body.

> *"Thinking is the biggest mistake a dancer could make. You should feel."*
> Michael Jackson

In China's Tang dynasty, many poets likened *wu wei* to the metaphor of being drunk. One poet compared someone inspired by *wu wei* to a drunk man who falls uninjured from a moving cart because he has freed himself from a more rigid and controlling mindset. Painters from the Tang period onwards made *wu wei* central to their practice. Rather than laboriously attempting to reproduce nature faithfully, the artist would find nature within themselves, surrender to its call and then let it flow out through the brush onto silk or paper.

This is how a Tang dynasty poet, Fu Zai, described the painter Zhang Zao in action: "Right in the middle of the room he sat down with his legs spread out, took a deep breath, and his inspiration began to issue forth. Those present were as startled as if lightning were shooting across the heavens or a whirlwind was sweeping up into the sky. The ink seemed to be spitting from his flying brush. He clapped his hands with a cracking sound. Suddenly strange shapes were born. When he had finished, there stood pine trees, scaly and riven, crags steep and precipitous, clear water and turbulent clouds. He threw down his brush, got up, and looked around in every direction. It seemed as if the sky had cleared after a storm, to reveal the true essence of ten thousand things."

All this was *wu wei*.

Doing nothing could be a strategic decision

> *"He will win who knows when to fight and when not to fight."*
> Sunzi (or Sun Tzu), Chinese military strategist
> who wrote *The Art of War*

General Vo Nguyen Giap was the Vietnamese military and political leader whose perfection of guerrilla warfare as well as conventional strategy and tactics led to the Viet Minh victory over the French (and to the end of French colonialism in Southeast Asia) and later to the North Vietnamese victory over South Vietnam and the United States. He knew that his army was no match for the powerful arsenal of the Americans. His strategy was one of guerrilla war, wait and see, hide when the enemy approaches, attack when the enemy is resting. The US military commanders were under intense pressure by the American public back home to end the war "by Christmas" and "bring our boys home." General Giap saw this as the soft underbelly of the Americans. He famously declared that his soldiers were prepared to fight the war for 100 years. The US had to withdraw ignominiously after many years of protracted warfare.

Slowing down to speed up

Here is another counter-intuitive idea. With the hyper-frenetic pace around us, how can anyone contemplate slowing down? One leader quipped, "I think you mean speeding up to speed up?" No, that's not it. It creates more confusion, misalignment and even greater complexity. Ironically, back in our school days, we were all taught the proverb, "More haste, less speed."

Here's how a leading agrichemicals company decelerated to accelerate. For the last few years, their Asian business had been clocking double-digit growth. This was great news. But they also knew that they had a lot of misalignment across the regions. Many of the country heads wanted to operate independently because they saw little value in collaborating with each other. There was lot of mistrust between the businesses and the support functions such as Operations, R&D, Finance, HR, EHS (Environment, Health and Safety).

A recent audit identified a series of financial irregularities and EHS violations. In some of the countries, some employees had suffered serious injuries, and there were court injunctions to cease operations. When all their senior leaders came together for a three-day offsite, the gravity of the situation became clear to all. They had to clean up their act individually and collectively. Achieving strong growth would not absolve them from non-compliance to the company's policies and regulations.

Despite initial resistance, they gradually slowed down to focus on what they had done well, what they had allowed to fall through the cracks, and what they now had to correct as the APAC Senior Leadership Team. They then committed to engage each other in sincere and open conversations and learn to build trust across the countries and functions. Their biggest learning was that there was so much interdependency that they could only succeed by working closely with each other.

Three months later, another internal audit survey showed that the leaders were now more in sync with each other. Businesses and the support functions were collaborating to put checks and balances in place. When individual leaders were interviewed, they mentioned that it was a transformational journey. By spending quality time to get to know each other and discuss tough issues, working processes were now aligned. In the past they were working against each other. Now they were working with each other towards a common set of targets. Their Regional VP concluded, "By slowing down to listen to each other and get coordinated, we speed up in our execution."

Summing up

How do we know whether we are in the flow, or still doing too much needlessly? A useful metaphor to consider is the rowing of a canoe in a river. If you are rowing upstream against the current, the feeling is inescapable. You expend a lot of effort that does not seem to bear fruit. Susanto was in this situation. But he was too busy to notice. If you are in the *wei wu wei* mode, you are paddling downstream. You are enjoying yourself, and people around you are flourishing as well. Things are coming together on their own.

Pause regularly, climb onto the balcony and look around you. Look inside yourself. Tap into the quiet wisdom of your body. How you feel will be an indication of where you are. Be ready to make the necessary changes in your mindset and habits if you wish to achieve more while doing less.

13

WE NEED STRESS, JUST NOT TOO MUCH

Be at your peak despite stress

"We now have scientific proof that the mind can heal the body."
Herbert Benson, Professor, Harvard Medical School

When we talk about stress, what we usually think about are its negative health impacts and that it is irredeemably bad. But the latest research at Stanford University shows that stress can make us stronger, smarter and happier – if we learn how to open our minds to it.

A balanced view of stress

Like many things in life, there are both beneficial and harmful effects of stress on performance. In 1908, two researchers, Robert M. Yerkes and John D. Dodson of Harvard Physiologic Laboratory, first calibrated the relationship between stress and performance in what is now dubbed the Yerkes-Dodson Law. As stress increases, so do efficiency, creativity and performance. But only up to a certain point.

From then onwards, as stress continues to build up, performance and efficiency decline dramatically. This is when the symptoms of excessive stress kick in. Stress-related disorders surface: people can't think clearly, mistakes pile up. Lapses of judgment occur and hostility sets in. In severe cases, panic, depression and insomnia follow, leading to a meltdown. This is the fight-or-flight response.

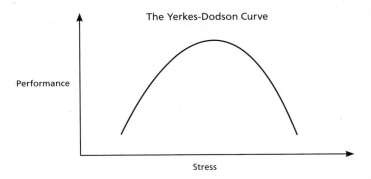

The Yerkes-Dodson Curve

Performance

Stress

The fight-or-flight response is the same ancient alarm that jump-started our hunter-gatherer ancestors into taking evasive action from aggressive animals. This is a built-in gift of evolution without which we humans won't be here today. But it is ill-suited for our modern life when the only threats are everyday events such as failing to meet a sales target or encountering a hiccup when doing a major presentation. Yet, our mind is so powerful that we can set off the alarm just by thinking ourselves into a frenzy. Many of us are chronically under stress as a result. And we don't know how to manage it. When the stress pattern becomes routine, the constant biochemical pounding takes its toll. Our body is ravaged. This leads to hypertension, heart attacks, strokes, diabetes and even cancer.

However, as business executives and top-flight performers have found out, stress can be a stimulus for outstanding performance. Good stress, also called eustress, energizes and spurs us to exceed our own expectations. There are also other upsides that a certain amount of stress can bring about:

- **Enhances motivation:** Under the pressure of a looming dead-line, it kick-starts motivation. People become more focused and find themselves more energized. Team members will prioritize and agree to put aside other matters to make sure the important pieces are completed on time. This promotes bonding and helps nurture trust between members.

- **Spurs creativity:** There is an old saying, "Necessity is the mother of invention." When we experience stress, our creative juices start flowing. We are also more willing to raise ideas that may seem impractical because time is running out and we need that last bit in the proposal. Be forewarned, though. Under extreme stress, people burn out and creativity is killed.

- **Builds resilience and encourages growth:** When people go through tough times and solve problems, they acquire confidence and skills that will serve them well in the future. With increased resilience, they now possess that inner belief that they can rise to the challenge the next time a tough one comes along.

  One simple mindset reset that can help us face and find the good in the stress in our lives is to view it as an opportunity to learn and grow. The ability to learn from stress is built into the basic biology of the stress response. For several hours after, the brain is rewiring itself to remember and learn from the experience. Stress leaves an imprint on your brain that prepares you to handle similar stress the next time you encounter it. Psychologists call the process of learning and growing from a difficult experience stress *inoculation*. Going through the experience gives your brain and body a stress vaccine. This is why putting people through practice stress is a key training technique for NASA astronauts, emergency responders, elite athletes and others who have to thrive under high levels of stress.

- **Makes our lives meaningful:** Paradoxically, a stress-less life will cause more problems down the road. When people have no goals in life and nothing to spur them on, they stagnate and drift along aimlessly. People need a sense of purpose. With purpose comes goal-setting and then pressure to meet those goals. Without this, why even get out of bed? The stress of meaninglessness is unbearably powerful. They grow old fast and succumb to many attendant health issues.

Leverage stress but don't be overwhelmed by it

Stress as we have discussed is a double-edged sword. It can make you a better person and it can also bring you down. To get the most out of our ambivalent relationship with stress, we need to be mindful of the way we lead our lives. There are three steps that may be useful:

1. **Be aware of it:** First, reframe the way you think about stress. It will be a constant companion, and if well attended to, it can enrich our lives. Each day we will experience stress. The question is how much and what's causing it. We can make it a habit throughout the day to pause and check in with ourselves. Do we feel our heart is racing? Our jaw is tight? Feeling out of control? What is our behavioral pattern? Short-tempered? Snappy? Can we stand up and walk away for a while to restore our balance?

2. **Own it:** Stress comes with the role that we play and the responsibilities that we have accepted. Imagine yourself living a stress-free life. Is that your dream? Some will say that's what they want. In your moment of frustration when the sky seems dark, maybe. But most of us are grateful to be under some stress. We know that we can handle it and that there are challenges that we are facing. So when stress comes, tell yourself it comes with the territory. Live with it and roll with the punches. Get better doing this every day.

3. **Manage it:** There is now scientific evidence that your mind and body are powerful allies. How you think can affect how you feel.

And how you feel can affect how you think. An example of this mind-body connection is how your body responds to constant worries over jobs, finances, or other problems. These cause tense muscles, pain, headaches and stomach problems. They may also lead to high blood pressure or other serious problems. And the reverse can happen. Constant pain or a health problem like heart disease can affect your emotions. You might become depressed, anxious, and stressed, which could affect how well you treat, manage, or cope with your illness.

Dr. Herbert Benson of Harvard Medical School is the pioneer of mind-body medicine. In the 1960s and 1970s, he and his team did break-through research proving that the mind can heal the body. He coined the term "relaxation response" or RR to describe a variety of mind-body techniques that trigger an anti-stress relaxation response.

"This means that you have the innate ability to self-heal diseases, prevent life-threatening conditions, and supplement established drug and surgical procedures with mind-body techniques that can improve your physiology, biochemistry, brain functioning, and genetic activity."
Dr. Herbert Benson

The basic elements of this technique have been known and used for millennia in many cultures, traditions, religions and ways of life throughout the world such as Christianity, Judaism, Islamic mysticism or Sufism, Hinduism, Daoism, Buddhism, Yoga and Shintoism.

These are the steps involved, essentially involving a breathing exercise:

1. Find a quiet place and sit in a comfortable position.
2. Pick a neutral word such as "one," a phrase, image or a short prayer. Or focus on your breathing.

3. Close your eyes.
4. Progressively relax all your muscles.
5. Breathe slowly and naturally. As you exhale, repeat or picture silently your word or phrase or simply focus on your breathing rhythm.
6. Assume a passive attitude. When other thoughts intrude, simply think, "Oh well" and return to your focus.
7. Continue with this exercise for an average of 15–20 minutes
8. Practice twice a day.

Clinical work by medical researchers has shown that the relaxation response is an effective therapy for anxiety, mild and moderate depression, anger, insomnia, hypertension and a host of other stress-related disorders. Specifically these are some of the benefits:

- Decreased metabolism, heart rate, blood pressure, and rate of breathing
- Overcoming the fight-or-flight response
- Increase in attention and decision-making functions of the brain
- Changes in gene activity that are opposite of those associated with stress

In addition to the breathing exercise, there are two more habits to build into your life:

1. **Eat and sleep well:** These are hygiene factors. Poor diet leads to weight and health issues. Lack of sleep will impact concentration and work efficiency. Together they loop back to the brain, kicking off a vicious cycle.

2. **An exercise routine:** The human body is meant to move. Sitting down for a long time throughout the day leads to serious health

hazards. Exercise does not need to be very strenuous. Thirty minutes five times a week of moderate activity will do wonders. If your body is healthy, you naturally become optimistic.

14

IN SEARCH OF A GREAT IDEA

Persist and persevere, then break away

*"Genius is 1 percent inspiration and
99 percent perspiration."*
Thomas Edison

All of us work hard at our job. But we frequently lament that we are stuck in a rut, trotting out the same tried-and-tested ways. With the environment changing so rapidly, what used to work in the past isn't going to cut it now. The pressure mounts. We huddle with our team to come up with an innovative idea for a marketing campaign. Or to solve a technical glitch that has shut down the factory. Or to make a pitch to a client looking to improve market share. Countless ideas and suggestions have been bandied around. They all seem logical. But none seems to be the solution that we are looking for. And time is running out. Stress is getting unbearable. What should we do?

How one leader abandons the struggle and makes a breakthrough

Undoubtedly we have encountered countless similar challenges. It gets to the point when we are so exhausted that we can't think any more. As one person, Liza, describes it, "My brain is fried." She decides to abandon her struggle, so to speak. Though it's late in the evening, she laces up her track shoes and goes for a long jog in her neighborhood. This is her usual routine to destress and regain her sense of balance. It isn't uplifting for the first few kilometers. The ideas and concepts are still swirling in her head, all competing with each other. Liza persists, nonetheless. Then she feels her body relaxing and a sense of calmness. At the end of her jog, she takes a long slow walk home. Nothing has changed. It seems like just another runner's high. After a warm bath, Liza slips into bed, and sleeps soundly. The next morning she feels rejuvenated and peaceful. The jumble of ideas that had been at war in her mind have made peace with each other. There is now a connecting strand that stands out clearly. When she reaches the office, Liza eagerly shares her epiphany with her team members. This is precisely what they have been looking for. With great excitement, they rework their presentation. After lunch, Liza and her colleagues meet up with the client. They are awarded the contract at the end of the presentation.

The Breakout Principle

Dr. Herbert Benson, whose pioneering work on the Relaxation Response (RR) we discussed in the previous chapter, has found that we can use stress productively by applying the "breakout principle." This leverages the paradoxical dynamic between good and bad stress as defined by the Yerkes-Dodson Curve. In the space between the two lies the possibility that we can regulate stress, avoid burnout and raise our performance. It is a simple and scientifically proven technique that many leaders and their organizations have applied to manage stress and unleash greater job satisfaction.

> *"As a scientist, I guard against wild promises. But my research and study have convinced me that the Breakout Principle does indeed transcend other self-transformation claims, to the point that it constitutes a kind of ultimate self-help principle that can carry you to significantly new levels of performance and achievement."*
> Dr. Herbert Benson

There is a distinct four-stage process:

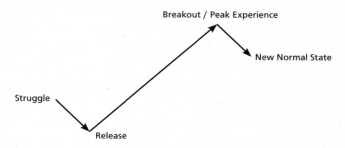

Stage 1: The struggle. First and foremost, no breakout is possible without first investing a lot of time and effort. This is not a scheme to become successful without really trying. Imagine grappling with a particularly intractable problem – to develop a vaccine to tackle the Covid-19 virus, a new approach to alleviate severe traffic congestion in the metropolis, deciding who to hire between two outstanding job candidates, etc. In the run-up to making a judgment call, there has been tons of data, analyses ad nauseam, endless debates and never-ending new inputs. Compounding the problem is that it involves many people, all with different areas of expertise and hence perspectives. First it is exciting. Then it becomes nerve-racking as the days and even weeks flash by. Stress is relentlessly creeping up the Yerkes-Dodson curve.

Stage 2: The release. It soon reaches a point when you can't think straight anymore. The sensations are unmistakable. You start to fidget. You can't keep still. Your team members are looking at each other as if in a daze. You are all spinning around in a loop. Should you surrender temporarily and take a break? A walk, a jog, play with the kids, go swimming, watch a movie, just close your eyes and meditate. Or sleep in exhaustion. You can't short-change this. Be willing to take some time off. Could be a few hours. A weekend. Or even weeks. Writers who encounter "writer's block" may be unable to continue for an indefinite period of time.

As Liza discovers, her mode of surrender unconsciously disrupts the swirl of ideas spinning round in her head. Billions of neurons fire in different patterns. Seemingly disparate and contradictory thoughts start to coalesce into one connected whole. As the brain quietens down, a series of biochemical explosions will bubble up inside our body and brain. Benson attributes this to the release of increasing amounts of nitric oxide through the body. There is also a remarkable calming of the body and mind as shown by fMRI (functional magnetic resonance imaging) graphs.

> *"In the eye of the storm,*
> *Can you stay centered and calm?*
> *Having done all that is possible,*
> *Can you sit and let go?"*
> Laozi

Stage 3: Breakout/Peak experience. This is when the breakout occurs – the Eureka moment at the end of a grueling journey. Elite athletes, artists and dancers reach this state when they train hard and let go and allow the spirit of the moment to take charge. Psychologist Mihaly Csikszentmihalyi calls it the *flow*. When flow occurs, the ideas all come together congruently and effortlessly.

Stage 4: The new normal. The breakout cycle ends by creating a new baseline for performance. This means that the struggle is remembered and leaves the person in a stronger position to elicit breakouts in future. The more the habit of eliciting breakout is practiced, the more natural it will become.

Now let's examine how the Breakout Principle maps onto a well-known model of creativity.

The four stages of creativity

In 1926, the psychologist Graham Wallas shared his famous model of creativity, a way of understanding how original ideas form in the mind and are carried into the world. These are the four stages of the model:

- **Stage 1: Preparation.** This is the perspiration part that Thomas Edison referred to. It is a lot of hard work involving thinking, brainstorming, fact-gathering, researching and experimentation. Without this, the seeds of a great idea will not be planted.

- **Stage 2: Incubation.** This is rather mysterious. It is when the investigator abandons or surrenders the ceaseless search for the elusive answer and allows his subconscious mind to take over.

- **Stage 3: Illumination.** It is at this stage that the Eureka moment arrives. This is what the investigator has spent days, week or months in quest of.

- **Stage 4: Implementation.** Here's when you start to evaluate your idea and determine how good it is.

As you will have noticed, Benson's Breakout Principle maps onto Wallas's Creative Process perfectly.

Some well-known examples of creativity

In the following examples we'll take a look at the various ways creatives achieve their breakthroughs. As we have discussed, the initial stage of enormous and backbreaking hard work is mandatory. The payback will come through the Illumination stage. While some of the people we feature here were lone wolves, in our modern era breakthrough ideas will require collaboration with co-workers and even cross-disciplinary pollination of ideas.

- **Countless ordinary men and women:** These are people from all walks of life. They may be known to you. They may even include you. Whatever they are doing, they will have encountered seemingly insurmountable difficulties that they have found a way of creatively resolving. A chat with them will reveal that intuitively and even unknowingly, their breakouts are preceded by enormous hard work, exploration and experimentation. When the right idea finally strikes, it will have come during some form of incubation or release. Think back. Has it occurred to you before? Now that you understand the process, how can you apply it to your work and life?

- **Charles Dickens:** Taking long walks around London was Charles Dickens's preferred mode of incubation. A few minutes' stroll can indeed increase blood flow to the brain, which can boost creative thoughts. Dickens wrote his novels between the hours of 9 am and 2 pm. After that, he would go out for a long walk. He once said, "If I couldn't walk fast and far, I should just explode and perish."

- **Paul McCartney:** The Beatles' classic ballad "Yesterday" has a dreamy and gentle melody, with lyrics that feel plucked out of a man's deepest subconscious. According to rock legend Paul McCartney, he came up with the earliest stages of the song in his sleep. When he woke up, he let them be poured out of his soul on the piano next to his bed.

- **Twyla Tharp:** She is one of America's greatest choreographers. A daily exercise ritual is her secret to sustained creativity. Twyla Tharp says that she knows her day will be a productive one by waking up at 5:30 am, putting on her workout clothes and hailing a cab to the gym. Once she does that, all will be well.

- **Dmitri Mendeleev:** Russian chemist Dmitri Mendeleev was fascinated by the basic chemical elements. His deepest wish was to find a better way of organizing them. With his contemporaries discovering new elements at a rapid rate, he became convinced that there was some natural order underlying their existence

– some definitive pattern. Distraught by his inability to unlock this elusive order, Mendeleev took time away from his studies to vacation with his family, hoping the distraction would give new life to his fruitless investigations. This led to his discovery of the Periodic Table – one of the most iconic symbols in science. He said, "In a dream I saw a table where all the elements fell into place as required. Awakening, I immediately wrote it down on a piece of paper."

- **Werner Heisenberg:** German physicist Werner Heisenberg, one of the pioneers of quantum physics, achieved the breakthrough in his thinking during a two-week absence from the University of Göttingen to recover from an illness. He traveled alone to a remote archipelago on the North Sea and was doing nothing but taking daily walks and going for long swims when the bewildering intricacies of quantum theory formed clearly in his mind.

15

UNDERSTANDING YOUR COMPANY'S CULTURE

Seek first to understand, then adapt

"It is not the strongest of the species that survives,
nor the most intelligent that survives. It is the one
that is most adaptable to change."
Charles Darwin

One of the first things you need to do when joining a company is to find out about its culture and adapt to it. Many of us have come across instances of talented people hired from outside who stumbled rather badly in the first few months and never recovered. Then there are internal transfers such as high potentials posted from one country to another as part of their leadership development program. They may also encounter speed bumps. But those who devote time to reading the cultural tea leaves will find that the time spent in discovering the lay of the land is well worth it.

Why does this happen? Probably there are two contributing factors. Most companies overlook the importance of their corporate culture when onboarding newcomers. Layer onto this the rush to action in the so-called first 90 days that may wrong-foot them.

What is corporate culture?

While there is agreement that corporate culture exists and that it influences behaviors, there isn't a universally agreed definition about culture. It's like leadership. Hundreds exist. They have evolved over the decades and are all different from each other.

Culture refers to "the way things are done around here." Though unspoken, people who are in the company long enough know implicitly what is encouraged, discouraged, accepted or rejected. When properly aligned with personal values, drives and needs, culture can unleash tremendous energy towards a shared purpose and foster a high-performance climate. A strong culture is a common denominator among the most successful companies. Culture and strategy are inextricably linked, and there is a saying that "culture eats strategy for breakfast." In one study by Alex Edmans of London Business School involving 28 years of data, it was found that firms with high employee satisfaction (a key outcome of a strong culture) outperform their peers in long-run stock returns: 89% to 184% cumulative.

Decoding your company's culture

These are five dimensions of culture that will provide clues on how to navigate your new surroundings:

1. Values: What are values that the company espouses? Examples: Shared Purpose, Integrity, Trust, Customer-Centricity, Collaboration, Diversity & Inclusiveness, Empowerment, Openness. You may see these values boldly displayed on posters on the walls. Watch how they are put into practice daily. Do the senior leaders role-model them? How do colleagues exhibit them in their interaction with one another? Especially when they have differing perspectives, or when their functional objectives are in conflict. There will be situations in which what people say and do are not in sync with the company values.

Diversity in the workplace refers to intentionally employing individuals of varying gender, religion, race, age, ethnicity, sexual orientation, education, and other attributes – and very importantly, encouraging and allowing diverse opinions to be expressed. In many Western companies, the senior leadership ranks are heavily populated by Westerners. Women are also excluded. Likewise, many Asian multinationals prefer people of their same nationality. Look out also for signs about the balance between individualism versus team orientation. At meetings do people use "I" or "We" predominantly?

2. Behaviors: What do you notice of the way people behave towards each other? Informal and friendly? Helpful and respectful? Patient and caring? Official and unwelcoming? Observe how people interact with others up and down the hierarchy. Do people speak openly when they have opinions that aren't mainstream?

What do managers focus on in their day-to-day work? What are their priorities? Task orientation vs people orientation? Or both? Do managers provide feedback and coach their people? Who are the managers who are admired? Those who are feared and disrespected? Who are people who are influential and well regarded by others? What factors contribute to their influence? Who are the forces for good, and the up-and-comers? We've discussed corporate politics in an earlier chapter. What are you noticing?

Reach out and make friends with colleagues. They can provide you the inside scoop. You will be able to sense the vibes. They are unmistakable. How is the energy level? Is there optimism and a can-do spirit? Do people crave challenges? Or do they put their heads down and stay out of trouble? When something bad happens, do people speak about them and then constructively work to resolve them collaboratively? Or is there finger-pointing and scapegoating?

How open is the company to change? There is an irony that may be a trap for unwary new hires. Highly talented people are brought in from the outside and told to shake things up and challenge the status quo. This may be an indirect way of telling you that the company is resistant to change. Tread carefully. During the onboarding program, if there is one, find out more about the company's attitude to change. What are the changes that have been implemented of late? By whom? What was the process adopted? If you misread or ignore the cues, you may not have the support that you will need to move ahead. And in the worst case, you may be left high and dry. Certain processes have become institutionalized for reasons you may not know. Some entrenched and powerful insiders may have been the champions. You may be the unwitting proxy of their opponents who want such processes to be replaced.

3. Communication: When people communicate with each other, what means do they prefer? Face-to-face? Emails? Pick up the mobile and speak? WhatsApp or WeChat? Is it usual to walk up to a colleague and have a casual chat? Are bosses' doors always open? More importantly, do they welcome you to drop in for a discussion?

How communication is conducted will shine a spotlight on the do's and don'ts that will determine your success in putting your ideas across. It may speak to the existence of deep hierarchy that inhibits open exchanges. Or it may signal an environment where the primacy of worthy ideas, and not job titles, holds sway.

4. Ways of working: Ways of working is an expression that encompasses three critical practices that have the potential to either lift the company to greater heights or cause it to sink to its knees in a morass of life-sucking and meaningless activities. These are: the way meetings are conducted; how conflict is managed; and how decisions are made.

Participate and observe how meetings are conducted. Watch the dynamics of attendees. What is their body language as they come into the meeting? Are meetings productive? During the discussions, do attendees have equal opportunities to speak up? When there is a polarity of views, how are opposing views expressed and reconciled? Is there a process for identifying and resolving conflict? How are decisions made? Do people support the decisions made collectively after different views have been heard and debated? Another important aspect of decision-making is whether there is bias for action or bias for analysis.

5. Subcultures. All organizations can have a mix of subcultures in addition to the dominant culture. Subcultures may exist among functions who, due to their responsibilities or expertise, may have institutionalized their own discipline and work processes. Though these may not be shared by the rest of organization, they can deepen and underscore the company's core values. Subcultures can also cause serious problems.

The audit or compliance departments may be very rule-based and will not condone deviations from company policies. In contrast, sales and marketing teams tend to be more flexible and ready to adapt to customer requests. Regional cultures often differ from the overall culture that HQ wishes to instill. A case in point is the centralized management approach at one huge company. When it started to venture into China, India and Brazil, it encouraged a more decentralized system to be more agile in these economies. Another example is a Dutch company with its emphasis on egalitarianism. In Asia, where the national cultures emphasize hierarchy, some adjustments had to be made.

Moving forward

After three months, sit back and reflect. These are some questions to consider:

- How would you describe the dominant culture in your company in three different phrases? What are the subcultures? How different are they from the dominant culture?
- What are the key differences between the cultures in your new and old companies?
- How aligned are the company's values with your values?
- What practices will come naturally to you? What are those that you need to consciously adapt to?

- Who are the role models that you may want to observe and learn from?

Do bear in mind that when you join a new company, your previous achievements don't allow you to act outside of the norms of the culture you are now in. Refrain from making comparisons and holding up certain practices in your former company as best-in-class. You have already been hired because of your track record elsewhere and the potential benefits you will bring. Your future success will be determined by your impact in the new environment, and how well you adapt yourself.

16

LEADING ACROSS CULTURES

**Navigating cultural differences skillfully
is a prerequisite for success**

"Strength lies in differences, not in similarities."
Stephen Covey

Working alongside people of cultural backgrounds different from yours is a given these days in business. They could be peers, bosses and team members. You may encounter the same with clients, business partners or vendors. This doesn't just happen because you have relocated to another country. You may already be experiencing this in co-located or virtual settings. Recognizing cultural differences and learning how to navigate them skillfully is a prerequisite for survival and success. Consider the following four cases:

Case 1: At the global management meeting of a US multinational, these were the attendees: the American president and 10 VPs – 5 Americans, 3 Europeans and 2 Asians. There were lots of exchanges among the Americans and the Europeans. But the two Asians were rather quiet. Each gave an obligatory 30-minute update. After that they said nothing. That evening, the president invited the Chinese and Japanese VPs for a drink at the bar. He asked them why they were silent during the session. Both men felt rather awkward about this question. But after a few more beers, they said that there was no opportunity to speak up. Their Western peers were dominating the meeting. The president replied that he expected all to share their ideas, and even offer differing views. Nobody should wait to be invited to speak. It was a given that participants should be scrappy and assertive. He would like all his colleagues to treat the meeting as a forum for open discussions and a touchpoint to bring their collective thinking to a higher level. It was every leader's responsibility to go beyond his immediate realm of accountability and provide insights that others may benefit from. If everyone kept within his comfort zone, it would lead to silo thinking and subpar business performance. And with APAC's revenue now approaching parity with America's, the two Asian VPs should seize the opportunity to request for much more time on the agenda.

Question: Why do Westerners and Asians behave so differently in business meetings?

Case 2: Jenny is the Singaporean Sales VP overseeing a high-powered team of retail directors of diverse cultures in the ASEAN (Association of Southeast Asian Nations) zone. They are Thai, Malaysian, Indonesian, Indian, French, Italian and Dutch, leading numerous stores in the various countries. Their team dynamics are an interesting sight to behold. The Asians express their opinions calmly, politely and confidently while making sure nobody loses face. The Europeans adopt the opposite tack: confrontational, uncompromising and challenging everybody, including Jenny. But no one takes offense or feels intimidated, though. The debates are thorough and constructive. Year over year, the ASEAN zone outperforms other regional teams.

Question: What is the secret sauce of their success?

Case 3: Two American executives flew to Frankfurt to meet up with a small German telecommunications firm. The aim was to finalize a technology joint venture. A few video conferences had taken place in the last three weeks. An MOU (Memorandum of Understanding) had been exchanged. The meeting started at 9 am. By 4 pm, the Americans felt that they had nailed down all the important details. They requested for the contract to be signed. The Germans, however, were clearly feeling nervous. They weren't ready to proceed.

Question: Why did the Americans and the Germans react so differently at the closure of the meeting?

Case 4: It is Chen Lu's opportunity to present his ideas to the executive leadership team located in San Jose. This takes place before the coronavirus pandemic so it is an in-person meeting. Chen from Beijing is the company's leading expert in robotics technology. It is his first high-level presentation and he is visibly nervous. Nonetheless, he is widely respected, has a firm grasp of the subject and his recommendations are eagerly awaited by the audience. The setting is rather informal. Apart from Chen, all the people present are Americans. While waiting for the meeting to start, there is a lot of light banter and wisecracks about last Sunday's Super Bowl game. Chen feels a little left out as he is unfamiliar with American football.

When Chen's turn comes, he tees up his presentation by first sharing data supporting his recommendations. He has not finished his fifth slide when the audience starts to ask questions. They are coming fast and furious, and he soon gets the impression that they want him to cut to the chase and zoom in on his conclusions and recommendations. Chen is unfazed. He takes the cue and skips all the slides on data and research. The next 20 minutes are devoted to his recommendations. At the end of it all, he receives endorsement on his proposal without much difficulty.

Question: What can we learn from Chen's deft handling of his American colleagues' line of inquiry?

Understanding cultural differences

If you were the protagonists in the four scenarios, how would you have made sense of the ways people from the various cultures operate? Many researchers and scholars such as Hofstede, Trompenaars, Javidan, Molinsky and Meyer have studied this fascinating topic over the decades. Erin

Meyer at INSEAD has written a book entitled *The Culture Map: Breaking Through the Invisible Boundaries of Global Business*. I highly recommend this as a resource. In the following discussions, I've adapted Meyer's Culture Map to take our explorations a little deeper.

In the framework, I have selected six dimensions that capture the salient cultural differences that can help us navigate across cultures more dexterously. Each dimension consists of two opposing behaviors that serve as bookends on a spectrum. The various cultures in the world are arrayed at different points on this spectrum relative to each other. To avoid cluttering the chart, only the countries mentioned in the case studies will be highlighted.

The Culture Map

The six dimensions of cultural differences

1. Individualism vs Collectivism. Individualism stresses individual goals, rights and interests. The United States is the most individualistic nation in the world. Americans are more likely to prioritize themselves over a group and they value independence and autonomy. They are more outspoken and will actively influence others to their points of view. Many European countries will also lean towards individualism but are a little less so than the Americans. On the other hand, collectivism sees individuals as members of a larger whole. There are social norms to ensure that harmony and the greater good are prioritized over individual needs. People in such countries are conscious of the impact of what they say and do in the larger community. Hence they will not speak out of turn, and prefer to keep their views to themselves. Countries such as China, Japan, Korea, India and those in Southeast Asia, the Middle East and Africa have a collectivist culture.

2. Communication. In some cultures, people say explicitly and clearly what is on their mind. You can take whatever they say at face value. When carried to the extreme, it leaves listeners wondering whether the art of communication will be better served with a little subtlety. Other cultures may communicate in a more nuanced and layered way. Messages are often implied but not plainly stated. On this dimension, direct and indirect styles will be the extreme poles. Americans and Germans are direct communicators while Chinese, Japanese and Koreans are indirect communicators. Messages are conveyed implicitly, requiring the audience to "read the air", so to speak. Somewhere in the middle will be the French, English, Russians and Italians. The relative positions of countries to each other are important. Thus, French, English, Russians and Italians, occupying the middle spots, are slightly less direct in their communication styles than the Americans and Germans.

3. Managing disagreement. Although in principle we all agree that a diversity of views will lead to better solutions, countries around the world have different ways of managing it. There are two opposite preferences: confrontational and conflict-avoidant. The confrontational approach views open disagreement positively. By stating differing opinions and arguing the pros and cons, a better understanding of the situation will ensue. The conflict-avoidant approach prefers to focus on common areas of interest and not accentuate areas of disagreement. This is to maintain good relations and preserve goodwill. Israel, Germany, Netherlands and France have a confrontational culture. Japan, Korea and China are conflict-avoidant. USA and UK are around the middle of the spectrum.

4. Leadership. This dimension discusses to what extent people accord deference to authority figures. It places countries on a spectrum from egalitarianism on the left to hierarchical on the right. Denmark, Netherlands, Israel are on the extreme left. USA, UK, Germany, France and Italy occupy the middle positions. Japan, Korea and China are placed on the extreme right. What this means is that in countries toward the left, there are more robust exchanges and challenges between leaders and the people who work for them. Leaders are not revered and do not expect to have their people accept everything they dish out. Towards the right end, there is much respect for bosses. People are reluctant to speak up even if they don't agree with their supervisors. The hierarchy is very deep, and relationships are formal.

5. Trust. There are two ways in which trust is built and earned – through tasks or relationships. The extreme left is occupied by task-based societies. Trust is built cognitively through results accomplished. At this end, whether we decide to trust the other party depends on how well the work has panned out and the delivery of results per commitment. The US and Western Europe are task-based societies. In relationship-based societies, trust is earned through weaving strong affective connections. This means socializing through dinner, drinking and many rounds of golf. It is a form of due diligence, if you will. If you really want to know the real person, peek behind the mask, before agreeing to a partnership. This is a very slow and time-consuming process. Only then will trust be established. Saudi Arabia, Nigeria, China, India and Japan are relationship-based countries. But it doesn't mean that performance is not considered. After getting to know each other, the relationship-based people will be on the lookout for evidence that the parties that they agree to work with will deliver per commitments.

6. Persuasion. There are two styles of reasoning in the Western hemisphere: principles-first versus applications-first. Most people are capable of practicing both forms of reasoning, but their preferred pattern of reasoning is heavily influenced by their culture's educational structure, as well as historical, religious and philosophical traditions.

In principles-first reasoning (sometimes referred to as deductive reasoning), it is expected that we start with providing a detailed explanation with facts and data that will be the foundation for our recommendations, i.e. prove the principle. Only then should we proceed to make our recommendations. In other words, explain why before going on to what and how. The principles-first approach, occupying the left side of the scale, is taught in school systems in Latin Europe (France, Italy, Spain, Portugal), the Germanic countries (Germany, Austria) and Latin America (Mexico, Brazil, Argentina). Such cultures are well-grounded in the dialectic process, which is parallel to the linear thinking approach we discussed in the introduction to this book.

In contrast, with applications-first reasoning (sometimes called inductive reasoning), individuals are trained to begin with a fact, statement, or opinion and later add concepts to back up or justify the recommendations as necessary. The preference is that you begin your message with an executive summary. Approach the discussions in a practical and concrete manner. In a business meeting, stay away from theoretical, academic and philosophic discourses. In other words, focus less on the why and more on the what and how. In general, Anglo-Saxon countries like the United

States, the United Kingdom, Australia, Canada and New Zealand are applications-based cultures, occupying the right side of the scale.

A common source of frustration encountered by subordinates of American bosses is that Americans tell them what to do without explaining why. From the perspective of the people in Latin Europe, Germanic countries and Latin America, this can feel demotivating, unintellectual and even disrespectful. By contrast, American bosses feel that when too many questions are asked, these subordinates are being uncooperative.

An example of the applications-first approach that may work with Americans is to start with a general observation such as, "In late April 2021, the Suez Canal was choked off by a giant container ship, throwing the world's supply chain into disarray. Our business is similarly very vulnerable as we are 100% dependent on two suppliers in China." This then leads to the recommendation, "We need to consider qualifying a third source in Southeast Asia." Once the audience's interest is piqued, the necessary details can be fleshed out.

In Asia, people embrace both applications-first and principles-first reasoning. While Asians are avid learners and are always trying to get the basics right before taking any course of action, they are keenly aware that it is a competitive environment out there. Hence, they first seek to investigate and understand. But beyond a certain point, they will readily act without second-guessing themselves. This exemplifies the circular thinking or holistic approach that was highlighted in the introduction to this book. Asians adopt the both-and philosophy and have little difficulty embracing both schools of thoughts.

Applying the Culture Map

Case 1: Why do Westerners and Asians behave so differently in business meetings? On both scales of individualism vs collectivism and communication, the US is on the extreme left while Japan and China are on the extreme right. This will explain why Americans are all ready to speak their minds freely. Germans, English, Italians and French, though a little less individualistic than Americans, will have no problem participating. The Japanese and Chinese, placed on the extreme right, will be naturally reticent. It is not unusual for them to remain silent unless a question or a request is posed to them.

Asians need to realize that such a cultural habit does not stand them in good stead. In a meeting with Westerners, they will short-change themselves by not sharing their thoughts. The impression given is that they lack confidence and aren't able to engage in the cut and thrust of business debate. Silence is decidedly not golden in this context. Asians have to get out of their own self-imposed cultural barrier. They need to find their voice in multicultural settings. Though it is not easy, with courage and persistence, they will soon be able to speak spontaneously with impact. This is key to developing leadership presence.

Western colleagues who tend to dominate discussions can be a little more encouraging to their Asian peers. Create some space and invite them to share their views. They may surprise you with well-considered ideas and suggestions.

Case 2: The secret sauce of Jenny's high-performing multicultural team. On the scale of disagreeing, Europeans will not hesitate to disagree with each other and their Asian colleagues. There is no disrespect intended, though. Jenny and the other Asians who are familiar with the European styles of expressing their points of views are comfortable sparring with them. Why? They have become adept in leading cross-culturally. This enables them to feed off each other's energy and ideas, co-elevating the team to think and lead at a higher level. When diversity is embraced, the team's collective intelligence is raised.

Case 3: Why Germans may take more time than Americans to warm up to potential business partners. In Case 3, the dimension at play is trust. The Americans, being very task-based, think that the few video calls, an MOU and now the face-to-face discussions should suffice to confirm that there is indeed mutual trust and goodwill on both sides. This is where it gets interesting. A country's position on these cultural dimensions relative to each other matters. If you notice, on the trust scale Germans are relatively less task-based than the Americans. They lean a little more to relationship-building. They need more time to do this, and hence demurred at the last moment in signing off on the deal.

Case 4: How Chen Lu wins over his American colleagues by adapting to their thinking style. It hasn't taken long for Chen Lu to sense that he has started off on the wrong footing by trotting out all the facts and figures. His America colleagues are anxious to get to the bottom-line. Without missing a beat, he zips to the last few slides and gives them what they prefer. Upon reflection after the presentation, Chen realizes that he had assumed that it was only logical for him to build his case gradually from the ground up. But when the audience got impatient, he quickly changed tack. His original approach would have worked well with a European audience.

Developing cultural versatility

How can you become more culturally savvy? Here are a few steps to consider.

First, understand where you are on the six dimensions discussed. Your position relative to people you have to interact with is key. Another important point is that a country's position on the Culture Map indicates a weighted average for people from that country. For instance, on the dimension of disagreeing, there may be outliers from China and Japan who are outspoken and willing to argue their cases, especially among Millennials. In a similar vein, there are Germans and Americans who are quiet and soft-spoken.

Second, reflect on how you tend to behave. Will this go down well with the other cultures? How then will you adapt? As the saying goes, when in Rome do as the Romans do. If your American colleagues are football fans, making an effort to understand this sport may help to break the ice. For Westerners trying to adapt to Asian cultures, taking an interest in Asian customs, traditions and cuisines may help.

Third, be curious and humble. Reach out to and show genuine interest in understanding other cultures. Observe, ask and listen. Share a little about your background and tell them that you are new to their culture and keen to learn and adapt. Look for allies in the group you are working with. Check in with them informally to find out how others are interpreting what you say and do. You can take it as a given that you will make mistakes when working across cultures. It's when you are out of your comfort zone that you will learn and adapt.

17

LEADING IN THE DIGITAL AGE

**We can't continue leading the way we
have been used to in the past**

*"Our hard skills will be eclipsed by AI, while our soft
skills will become ever more important."*
Panelists at WEF 2020

At the World Economic Forum (WEF) in 2016, Klaus Schwab described
the advent of the Fourth Industrial Revolution that the world has entered.
In his words, "The First Industrial Revolution used water and steam power
to mechanize production. The Second used electric power to create mass
production. The Third used electronics and information technology to
automate production. Now a Fourth Industrial Revolution is building on
the Third, the digital revolution that has been occurring since the middle
of the last century. It is characterized by a fusion of technologies that is
blurring the lines between the physical, digital and biological spheres."

It is evolving at an exponential rather than linear pace. And it is
disrupting almost every industry in every country. What used to be considered humans' strong suits – intelligence and expertise – will no longer
be so. Technologies are becoming smarter, faster and more powerful
while getting smaller, lighter and cheaper. For example, virtual robots
can be scaled at close to zero incremental costs and physical robots cost
a fraction of adding a headcount. In late 2016, the United States National
Science and Technology Council's Committee on Technology released a

report offering policy recommendations for dealing with machines' imminent capacity to "reach and exceed human performance on more and more tasks."

There is no denying that millions of jobs will be lost around the world, and countless people and their families will be left in ruins. If this sounds like an existential threat, it's because indeed it is. In 2020, the Covid-19 pandemic gave the world a foretaste of the widespread devastation that may be visited upon us for being ill-prepared for such a healthcare crisis. The impact of AI will be even greater and may never go away if we think back on the lessons learned from the first three industrial revolutions.

To overcome it, we must adapt and evolve into better versions of ourselves. Governments, corporations and think-tanks have an obligation to do a radical rethink of what the workforce can do. Educationists need to devise a new model of education that better prepares students for a global economy driven by artificial intelligence. Such new thinking will generate new social policies and human resource development agenda that emphasize innate human capabilities in the intersection between man and machines.

Leading in the digital economy

In organizations, there needs to be a paradigm shift in the way people are led. In the context of transformation, this must be driven right from the top. A 2020 study by the MIT Sloan School of Management captured its findings in a report entitled *The New Leadership Playbook for the Digital Age*. The first sentence of the report is a bold rebuke to those at the top of the current corporate food chain:

> *"Executives around the world are out of touch with what it will take to win, and to lead, in the digital economy."*

Leadership in the digital age will not resemble the leadership that organizations have come to know, love or loathe. Top-down, bureaucratic, bottom-line-driven hierarchies have no place in the new era. More lateral, collaborative, purpose-driven teamwork will be the norm.

The report surveyed over 4,000 global leaders about the future of leadership, and uncovered some startling data:

- Only 12% of those surveyed strongly felt that their leaders had the right mindset to lead them forward.
- Only 48% agreed that their organizations were prepared to compete in digitally driven markets and the digital economy.
- Less than 10% thought their leaders had the right skills to lead in the digital economy.

Competencies that today's workers must continue to develop

It is important for us to put things in perspective. The advances in science and technology have always been meant to better serve the needs of mankind. AI is not meant to make humans redundant, but to augment the capability of humans. For example, when customers are interacting with a human customer service agent, she may be AI-supported. The outcome is that the staff can spend more time on higher-value and higher-level tasks.

The ten competencies that are critical for the digital era are:

1. Complex problem-solving
2. Critical thinking
3. Creativity
4. People management
5. Coordinating with others
6. Emotional intelligence
7. Judgment and decision-making
8. Service orientation
9. Negotiation
10. Cognitive flexibility

These are innately human characteristics that can't be easily automated and will ensure that you will have a meaningful place in an

AI-suffused world. Here is brief discussion of such competencies that will still be in demand.

- **Interacting with other people:** People need and crave human contact. Even though great strides have been made towards affective computing, we are still a long way away from any technology that can genuinely recognize human emotions and respond appropriately. Any job that requires empathy such as primary care physicians, team leadership, teachers, caregivers and therapists will not be outsourced to technology any time soon. Human beings can build trust and rapport with each other, leading to a shared purpose. They can sort out diverse views and agree to act in alignment despite not completely buying into the final decision. Collectively, they can imagine the future, motivate and console each other, laugh together and celebrate each other's success. These require emotions that only humans possess. And human teams will continue to be in demand.

- **Systemic thinking:** In solving problems in society or organizations, there is even now a tendency to take a discipline-specific or siloed approach. This comes from our domain expertise. The net effect is that we can't really solve these problems, and may in fact create even more problems. We can, for instance, assemble a group consisting of engineers, software experts and data scientists. Chances are they will not speak to each other to hash things out. It's much harder to find someone who can draw all the threads together. This is the leadership and systemic thinking that all organizations need. AI can't do this.

- **Collaborative problem-solving:** Organizations now demand this in their managers and even entry-level positions. Some companies like Google define this as cross-functionality and even make it a cornerstone of their hiring process. They want deep specialists who can think and behave like generalists. Sounds paradoxical, doesn't it? Qualities such as curiosity, instinct for innovation and knack for working with others are much sought after. When people see the value of sharing their progress with each other regularly, they discover that what seems to be unrelated may in fact be closely connected by listening to each other. They also build their skills in conceptualizing, communication and synthesizing. This process often leads to serendipity (see Chapter 22).

- **Judgment calls on complex matters:** Robo advisers can quickly build a customer's investment portfolio. However, complex and emotionally difficult tasks can only be handled by humans as they bring contextual understanding, empathy and compassion to the interaction. In healthcare, AI will do the analytical work such as analyzing symptoms and mapping them against databases to perform diagnosis. But it will require a human doctor to make the final recommendation to the patients, taking into account their emotional state.

- **Critical thinking:** Briefly, we can say that critical thinking is the ability to solve problems, connect the dots on complex issues and provide a useful solution. Employers around the world will pay dearly for this capability in their hires. Machines are getting better at all the elements under the umbrella of critical thinking, but they have not grasped all of them. Take contextual understanding, for example. Human beings can read the nuances of dynamics in an organization that elude machines. This is situational awareness. They will factor this in when recommending a solution. This ability will remain a defining feature of human work.

- **Learning the new ABCs:** Arthur Yeung, senior management advisor at Tencent Group, puts it as follows: "All leaders need to be more technologically savvy. I come from HR, and I have been a deep specialist in that area. But today at Tencent, most of the important conversations center around technology. If I am going to be a trusted advisor to the top management team, I need to be in technology conversations. I need to go back and learn my ABCs: AI, Big Data, and Cloud."

At the January 2020 World Economic Forum in Switzerland, there was a panel discussion on "Reimagining Leadership in the Digital Age." Ben Pring, Director of Cognizant's Center for the Future of Work, sounded a wakeup call for "leaders who are out of touch" and "uncomfortable with technology." He continued, "Those who are clinging to older styles of leadership and don't have a passion for technology are soon going to be obsolete. Leaders don't necessarily need to be tech-savvy themselves but they do need to be turned on by technology, not turned off by it."

Many of the required skills have been discussed in this book. We'll now focus on emotional intelligence. Developing this will facilitate the acquisition of the other nine competencies.

What is emotional intelligence?

We have all met the two kinds of people who I'm about to describe. The first is highly intelligent, well educated and recognized for his technical mastery, whether in medicine, engineering or accountancy. In group settings however, his ideas don't travel far and he doesn't seem to have the influence befitting him. Then there is another person with solid – but not extraordinary – intellectual abilities and technical skills. He gets things done, works well with others and is enjoying recognition and success. What accounts for this difference?

Psychologists such as Daniel Goleman, John Mayer and Peter Salovey have spent decades researching this phenomenon. They attribute it to emotional intelligence. We have heard about this. It is also called EQ (emotional quotient). It is defined as the ability to be aware of our emotions in the moment, and to manage them so that we can positively impact our engagement with others. Why does EQ matter?

Here is a case study comparing two different styles of leadership. John and Sachiko are two highly regarded leaders in the same company. John is intense, task-oriented and impersonal. People respect him for his deep expertise in supply chain. Colleagues nickname him "The Hurricane" for his doggedness and single-minded determination to complete whatever he sets his mind to. Nothing will get in his way.

Sachiko is her company's go-to person for cross-functional projects. She knows that people are key to her success. She has said time and again, "We can achieve our common goals only when we are able to tap into our collective intelligence." She listens and leads quietly.

Think about both these leaders and their behavioral styles. Then try answering these two questions:

- Q1: Imagine you are working for both of them. How would you describe your experience with each person?

- Q2: Who will be more successful in their career? Why?

Do reflect and form an opinion about the two questions. In Chapter 18, we'll circle back and discuss this a little deeper.

The EQ framework

Emotional intelligence is made up of four domains:

1. Self-awareness is the ability to accurately perceive your emotions as they happen. This is the foundation of emotional intelligence. People who are self-aware know their strengths and weaknesses and their typical reactions to specific events, challenges and people. Take Tom, a marketing director. He is aware that numeracy is something he is not good at. When he is under the spotlight such as during a presentation or a meeting with senior leaders, he tends to sweat if there is a deep-dive

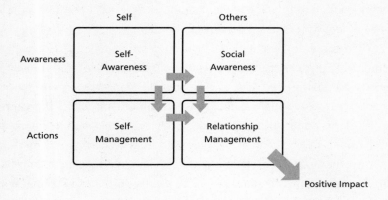

into a spreadsheet. Hence he will prepare ahead of time by having his finance manager role-play the Q&A with him. He makes it a point to request her to lead the financial analysis, while he helms the overall flow and the discussions.

2. Self-management is the ability to regulate your emotions so that you are behaving in a constructive manner. It is important to know what emotions are affecting us in the moment and to be able to regulate them in service of more important goals. Otherwise, we may come across as behaving inappropriately.

Being able to self-manage will also lead to adaptability, achievement-orientation and optimism. Consider your daily commute driving to the office. One day, you are running late for a client meeting. Another car veers dangerously into your path, nearly causing an accident. How will you react? Anger or calmness? Anger can lead to a heated exchange and possibly a collision. On arrival at the client's premises, the after-effects of the nasty incident will linger on. Calmness, on the other hand, gives you a sense of control. It's just carelessness on the part of the other driver, you reason. It can happen to you too. You brush off the incident and focus on your driving, arriving in good time, feeling purposeful and optimistic.

"Between stimulus and response there is a space.
In that space is our power to choose our response.
In our response lies our growth and our freedom."
Victor Frankl

3. Social awareness is the ability to sense what other people are feeling and understand what is going on. Underpinning this are two competencies: empathy and organizational awareness. It is akin to habitually having your antenna up when you are out there. There you are conversing with a few people, or immersed in a crowd of people. You listen and observe and take in the cues to sense the moods. You acknowledge other people's feelings when you are communicating difficult news. You reach out to people to better understand their perspectives. For instance, while facilitating a Zoom video conference with eight participants around the world, you pause once in a while to encourage questions. You wait patiently and create space for people to formulate their thoughts, being aware that cultural differences may hinder open communication. Even in virtual sessions, you are adept at reading the expressions on the participants' faces and intuit that some people need a gentle nudge to share their opinions.

4. Relationship management is the result of self-awareness, self-management and social awareness. It enables you to manage interactions positively. This comprises a complex set of competencies that include influencing, coaching and mentoring, conflict management, teamwork and inspirational leadership.

Take the case of a project team meeting. The team leader is absent as she has been called away urgently for another engagement. Everybody is feeling disgruntled and is using the time to share their gripes about the leader and her inability to rustle up cross-functional support for the project. For 30 minutes it goes on and so. Clearly this is not a productive use of time and everybody feels it. The atmosphere is one of grouchiness as well as a collective sense of guilt that the project is slipping. Then one member, sensing the frustration in the room, asks a question, "Now that we know what our issues are, what can we all do to help our project get back on track?" There is a pregnant pause. That question strikes a chord. The mood suddenly lightens up. Another person adds that as the leader is new to her job, let's all give her a helping hand. Gradually the narrative pivots towards the constructive. Emotions are contagious. They can gather greater momentum as they continue their present course. But a well-placed intervention at the right time can harness the pent-up energy and redirect it. A person with high emotional intelligence can do this.

Can emotional intelligence be developed?

Psychological research indicates that there is a genetic component to emotional intelligence. But work in leadership development programs has clearly demonstrated that emotional intelligence can be learned and developed.

A good way to start is to understand the EQ framework and the competencies under each of the four domains. Seek feedback through a 360-degree assessment which collects self-ratings and inputs from others who know you well. You get a rough gauge of your strengths and weaknesses. Examining the highest discrepancies between self-rating and other ratings will reveal blind spots and hidden strengths.

Now pick two behaviors to focus on and develop. Inform a few co-workers who know you well about your intentions to make changes. Work on these two behaviors over a period of six months at least. Ask for open and honest feedback on what changes they have observed in your behaviors. Thank them and continue your improvement journey. Soon others will sense the behavioral modifications that you are making. Your commitment to become a better version of yourself will rub off on them.

18

LISTENING AND QUESTIONING

Connect first, then lead

"I got to the top because I always had the right answers,
and suddenly I discovered that it's not about the answers.
It's about asking the right questions."
A top executive in a US multinational

When a new leader first appears, how do people decide whether they can trust her? According to social psychologists, our initial impressions of others essentially hinge on two characteristics. The first is competence: How capable, successful, and intelligent do we consider a person to be? The second is interpersonal warmth: How likeable or trustworthy does a person seem?

But which comes first, being competent or warm? A growing body of research shows that to influence and to lead is to begin with warmth. Prioritizing warmth helps you connect immediately with those around you, demonstrating that you hear them, understand them and can be trusted. Warmth in and of itself is not sufficient, though. A leader has to combine warmth with strength. The trust that people repose in the leader must also be earned by her ability to demonstrate competence.

Leaders should take this finding to heart: if they demonstrate high levels of "interpersonal warmth" first they will have a better chance at long-term success. A Zenger Folkman study that looked at 50,000 managers found that a leader's overall effectiveness is predicted more by warmth than competence.

> *"If you're seen as low-warmth, you have something like a 1-in-2000 chance to make the top quartile of effectiveness as a leader."*

There are two leadership skills that are instrumental in demonstrating warmth: listening and asking questions. Both have always been taken for granted and are under-appreciated. Most people appraise themselves as above-average in both areas. But reality does not bear this out.

Revisiting the case study on John and Sachiko

In Chapter 17, we described a case study involving two managers, John and Sachiko. In brief, here are some background details. John is intense, task-oriented and impersonal. People respect him for his deep expertise in supply chain. Colleagues nickname him "The Hurricane" for his doggedness and laser-like determination to complete whatever he sets his mind to. Nothing will get in his way. Sachiko is her company's go-to person for cross-functional projects. She knows that people are key to her success. She has said time and again, "We can achieve our common goals only when we are able to tap into our collective intelligence." She listens and leads quietly.

You were asked:

- Q1: Imagine you are working for both of them. How would you describe your experience with each person?

- Q2: Who will be more successful in their career? Why?

Both are real-life leaders who are commonly encountered in organizations. John prioritizes competence while Sachiko prioritizes warmth.

When colleagues of both persons are asked about their experiences working with them, these are the typical responses:

On John

- He is a real SME (subject matter expert). I have learned a lot from him.
- He tells me what I should do when I approach him for help. I do have questions and opinions, though. But I don't feel comfortable raising them.
- It is usually a one-way communication. From him to us. But there is no flowback from us to him.
- Good man. But he's not curious. He doesn't seem interested in hearing from the rest of us.
- I respect him as his recommendations are always sound.

On Sachiko

- She puts us at ease. We feel safe to share our views openly with her.
- The conversation is always two-way. If others are present, it is multi-directional. We feel engaged.
- We come into a meeting unsure of what to do. But at the end of it, we leave feeling more confident and empowered to act on our own. Strangely she does this without telling us what to do.
- She listens deeply. Sometimes she asks questions. It is quite magical. We gain clarity as we speak.
- Sachiko elevates our thinking. We see further and more widely.

When comparing notes about John and Sachiko, one senior leader who knows both very well says, "People who work with John feel that he is special. People who work with Sachiko feel that they themselves are special. We need more Sachikos in our company."

The transformative impact of listening

Like many capable people, John means well when he tells instead of listening. That's his way to provide value by sharing what he knows. And he enjoys playing the guru. In many of today's organizations, there is an addiction to being right: never be seen as being unsure! Be that as it may, John is unaware of the heavy price that he is paying when he adopts this as his primary mode of communication. Firstly, he casts himself as the guy with all the answers. While it is ego-boosting, it is also self-defeating. Expertise has a certain shelf-life, which is rapidly shortening. If knowledge is always flowing from him to others, he denies himself the chance to learn and take in new insights on how the world is changing. Additionally, it is a paternalistic relationship, which is disempowering.

Listening has the power of bringing people together, building mutual trust and self-respect, breaking down barriers that divide, helping both the speaker and the listeners to discover and understand, and expanding people's sense of self-worth. It is a magical, strange and creative force. Karl Menninger, long considered the elder statesman and dean of American psychiatry, said:

> *"The friends who listen to us are the ones*
> *we move toward. When we are listened to,*
> *it creates us, makes us unfold and expand."*

That's what Sachiko does. She listens with only one objective: understanding. Not to critique. Not to object. Not to convince. She intuitively realizes that people need space and permission to express their uncertainties and opinions. It is an intricate ritual. First, they hazard a tentative view. Then they wait for a reaction. If they feel that the environment is friendly and supportive, they will take the next step, and then the next. Others are also observing the dynamics. Leaders like Sachiko create an expansive climate for a rich conversation and self-discovery. They feel affirmed and empowered. And they realize that they have the tools to solve problems, so their bosses don't have to be the idea factory anymore.

How to be a better listener

- **Show respect:** Genuinely believe that each person has something unique to contribute. When they speak, give them your full attention. The respect shown to them will be reciprocated, and it will fuel an environment where good ideas routinely flow.

- **Be comfortable with silence:** When two old friends come together for a chat, or to take a walk through the woods, you will notice that their conversation is frequently punctuated by bouts of silence. Both remain relaxed and comfortable. When the conversation resumes, new ideas and perspectives emerge. The best thing we can do when there is silence is to stay calm and patient. This is when we can attend to the non-verbal cues from the other person. Is he relaxed or tense? What does his tone tell us? Words convey informational content. But what's the emotional content? Does he need a gentle nudge? Wait. He will resume when he is ready. This is generous listening.

- **Context is everything:** There is a maxim, "Where you stand depends on where you sit." Your role will shape your perspective on how the organization works and what is important to you. To appreciate why a person holds a certain point of view will require a contextual understanding. Putting oneself in others' shoes, i.e. being empathetic, will elicit greater appreciation of diverse opinions. When you know the context, the conversation becomes a journey of exploration and understanding.

- **Listen with the heart:** When you listen with the heart, you get more than what you are receiving through your ears and eyes. Sometimes, you sense that there is more to it than what the speaker is saying. If you look around, you become aware of non-verbal cues. How will you tease out the hidden messages?

Why we should lead with questions

Listening and questioning are a powerful combination. By asking questions at the appropriate moment, you can take the conversation to a deeper and richer level. For instance, when you sense that the speaker is offering a rather unusual suggestion, how do you respond? Show your surprise and remain silent? Be curious and encourage her to elaborate unfettered? Help her to clarify her assumptions? In any case, this is a pivotal moment. How you play it will define the trajectory of the conversation and those to come in the days and months ahead.

As people rise up the organization, the habit of telling instead of asking questions becomes ingrained in them. Telling is a quick way of getting things done. The greatest drawback of telling is two-fold: (1) The world is changing so fast that no one has a monopoly on correct answers, and there is no one right answer in any case; and (2) it inhibits others from being curious. Telling is a surefire way to suck the air out of a company.

The Nobel Prize-winning Jewish physicist Isidor Rabi once explained how his mother set him on the path to becoming a scientist. In most parts of the world, especially in Asia, every child coming home school will be asked by his mother, "What did you learn today?" But his mother asked instead, "Izzy, did you ask a good question today?" Judaism is a questioning religion. It teaches a child to be curious, to wonder, reflect, enquire. The child who asks becomes a partner in the learning process. To be without questions is not a sign of faith, but a lack of depth.

Whether you are an individual contributor, a team leader or a senior leader, you will need inputs from others. The quality of these inputs will determine the path that you walk. Some people constantly get told, "It's alright. It's all going well." And then a few days later, everything's wrong. Such leaders are trapped in a good news bubble. It is not uncommon to fall into this trap. Perceptive leaders are attuned to this phenomenon, and commit themselves to overcoming it. They do this by combining listening with questioning.

Finding the right questions

Formulating the right question is the difficult part. Someone once said that if you ask a stupid question, you will get a stupid answer. Framing the right questions is therefore the key. Unfortunately, formulating a great question does not come as easily as we wish. But you can get better and better at it by taking the following steps:

1. Connect first. We discussed this at the beginning of this chapter. Reach out widely and demonstrate warmth. Make it a point to wander around a little every day to run into different people not directly related to your line of work. This is an invitation to others to tell you things that they otherwise would not. Listen with curiosity. Your dialogue partners will unconsciously hint to you the follow-up questions that you should ask to bring the conversation to another level.

2. Develop a few questions that you will ask regularly. Arming yourself with these questions enables you to get the most out of the interactions with others. Your aim is to unearth opportunities, threats, divergent ideas. Continue to fine-tune these questions and observe their impact on others. Some reflection after the conversation will be useful. Some examples of questions are:
- What can we do differently?
- What is broken here?
- If you were me, what actions would you take?
- What can we learn from this?
- If you were leading this project, how would you approach it?

3. Use open-ended questions. Open-ended questions expand possibilities and thinking. They are defined by 5 Ws and 1H. Some examples:
- *What* is the impact?
- *Who* can we work with?
- *When* will the results be known?
- *Where* will this take place?

- *Which* is the preferred option?
- *How* should we define success?

We could add a 6th W question: *Why?* When asked appropriately, it unearths hidden assumptions.

Closed questions have the opposite effect. They shut down exploration as they allow only a binary response: yes or no. Example: Do you agree with this idea? A slight change of wording will make it more empowering: What do you think of this proposal? Or simply say, "Tell me more."

Sometimes, there is a need to probe to find out the root causes of a problem or to challenge assumptions. The "5 Whys" method that is part of the Toyota Production System is an excellent way to proceed. When trying to understand an event that has happened, start by asking "Why?". After hearing the response, ask another why, and then so on. By the time you reach the fifth why, the root cause is laid bare. You don't need to be an expert to be able to get to the bottom of things. Ironically, experts stop questioning themselves despite logical flaws that generalists pick up quickly.

The power of listening and questioning

Outstanding leaders are highly proficient in using both skills. They overlap, and at their intersection, their tensions nourish each other. Powerful questions do not arise if listening is inadequate. Listening may not be that useful if there aren't powerful questions. Here is a real-life case.

Julian is the newly appointed CIO (Chief Information Officer) in the APAC operations of an investment firm. The company has its HQ in London. Months before Julian joined the company, the senior members of his organization had already been recruited on his behalf. This was done by various functional heads at HQ. As the company is highly matrixed, Julian's organization structure is a mishmash of four sub-functions, each with solid line to him and dotted line to HQ, and operating in isolation from each other. It is, in his words, "a holy mess." For many months, Julian tries to meld them together, but to no avail. The heads of functions prefer to operate in their respective silos. In the meantime, the technology roadmap is still fragmented and nowhere ready for implementation. Julian is fast approaching his wits' end.

One day, he decides to speak to the APAC president, Zhang, to seek counsel. Zhang as his immediate supervisor has always been approachable, though Julian didn't feel ready to bring up this issue in previous conversations. Zhang listens quietly as Julian explains his dilemma. Julian tells Zhang that he feels trapped as the structure has already been frozen. He has tried to reach out to his peers at HQ but none of them will countenance any changes to their respective functions. It is silo thinking all the way from the top. Everyone suggests to Julian to tweak the other functions and leave theirs alone. What can Julian do?

After Julian has said his piece, Zhang asks, "What would you do if given a free hand?"

The response comes quickly, "I know what to do. But I don't have a free hand."

"What makes you think so?"

"There are too many strong parties who want to call the shots from a distance."

Zhang presses on. "If the old way with various people pulling the strings out of London is working, why appoint a new CIO?"

Julian, who came into the conversation feeling weighed down, now perks up. A flicker of a smile appears. In a blinding flash of the obvious, it dawns on him that it is his call. If he doesn't take charge, others will put their fingers in. When things turn awry, they will wash their hands of the matter.

The conversation has taken 30 minutes. Zhang listens the whole time. He poses only three questions. That's all it takes.

19

WE NEED MORE WOMEN LEADERS

Women leaders bring qualities that men leaders lack, and vice versa

"We have created a world where women are squeezed into just 25% – one-quarter – of the space, both in physical decision-making rooms, and in the stories that we tell about our lives. One-quarter is not enough."
Phumzile Mlambo-Ngcuka,
Executive Director, UN Women

Advancing women's equality in work and society represents one of the most sizable economic opportunities for the world. The 2015 McKinsey Global Institute report estimates that it can add $12 trillion to global growth. An additional $4.5 trillion a year can be added to Asia-Pacific GDP by 2025. This is 12% above business-as-usual. The largest absolute opportunity is in China at $2.6 trillion, a 13% increase. For India it will be an increase of $770 billion, which is the largest relative GDP growth. Across Asia-Pacific, 58% of the opportunity will come from raising the female labor-force participation ratio, 17% from increasing the number of hours women work, and the remaining 25% from more women working in higher-productivity sectors.

However, the path to parity is a long hard slog around the world. According to the recently published WEF 2021 Global Gender Gap Report, it will take an average of 135 years for women to reach parity on a range of factors. Examining data from 156 countries over 15 years, the report looks at four dimensions: economic opportunity, political power, education and health. Although there has been some progress in education and health, the statistics are sobering relating to higher economic hurdles, declining political participation, and workplace changes.

Women's markedly low representation in leadership positions is a global issue. According to McKinsey, slightly less than four women hold leadership positions for every ten men in business and politics worldwide. In Asia Pacific, there is only one woman in a leadership position for every four men. In some parts of East Asia, there are only 12 to 20 women leaders for every 100 men. This is a waste of talent that the region can ill afford, especially when many economies are aging, labor pools are eroding, and skills shortages are on the rise.

Stereotypes, biases and discrimination

Our general societal notion of leaders is that they are assertive, confident, rational, action-oriented, pragmatic and ambitious. These are masculine traits that are associated with men leaders. Viewing leaders through such a lens creates the classic double-bind that women face. A woman leader who exhibits feminine traits such as being compassionate, empathetic and collaborative may be viewed as too soft, a pushover or not decisive enough. Yet when she is as confident and aggressive as her male counterparts, people around her, including other women, criticize her as being bossy and unlikeable, triggering a backlash. Such gender stereotypes have throughout history legitimized leadership as the exclusive preserve of men.

In a fascinating study in the US Naval Academy published in 2018, researchers analyzed a large-scale military database (over 4,000 participants and 81,000 evaluations) to examine objective and subjective performance measures of leader performance. They discovered that the language in performance evaluation is applied differently to describe men and women. No gender differences were found in objective measures (e.g., grades, fitness scores, class standing). However, the subjective evaluations provided a wealth of interesting findings.

The researchers found significant differences in the assignment of 28 leadership attributes to men and women. Ten positive word were used to describe men, such as analytic, competent, athletic and dependable and so on, while only four positive attributes were assigned to women: compassionate, enthusiastic, energetic and organized. On the other extreme, only two negative words were assigned to men: arrogant and irresponsible. For women there were twelve negative words, such as inept, frivolous, gossip, excitable, scattered, temperamental, panicky, indecisive and so on.

These are not just words. They carry emotional undertones and have real-life implications for one's career and organizations. Language in performance evaluations tells us what is valued and what is not. The employees themselves who have such words applied on them know where they stand with their bosses and organizations.

Although both "analytical" or "compassionate" are positive characterizations, could one be more valuable from an organizational standpoint? To be analytical means that the individual is clear-headed, task-oriented, able to reason, interpret, strategize – all leading to driving the objectives of the business. Compassion is relationship-oriented, creating a positive work environment and building a healthy culture, but perhaps of lesser value to accomplishing business goals? When male bosses consider who to hire or promote, who are they more likely to pick? This is an irony here. When people are polled about the qualities of successful leaders, compassion is one trait that gets mentioned very frequently. Women leaders exhibit this quite naturally. And yet there is an unmistakable sense that it is not valued as much as masculine traits like being analytical or task-oriented.

Likewise, who do we retain or fire? A person who is arrogant may be abrasive and will impact the workplace negatively. But he may still be able to get the job done. On the other hand, an inept person is a lost cause and should be on the way out.

The most important takeaway from this study is that when most people are asked to picture a leader, what they see is a male leader. Even when women and men are equally effective as leaders, it's men who are seen as leaders, not women. The language that we use on male and female leaders is heavily influenced by stereotypes about their gender. In this era of talent management, diversity and inclusion initiatives, we are still trapped by our age-old biases, sending subtle messages to women that they aren't leaders.

The impact of women leadership on the workplace

As we have just seen, there are broad and deep-seated biases against women. The stereotypes against them have persisted for centuries. Even today they are unabated. But lots of research in the last few years has revealed compelling evidence that such biases are baseless and unwarranted. Here are two well-known studies.

Research 1: Women score higher than men in most leadership skills. Zenger Folkman is a highly respected US leadership consultancy founded in 2003 by Dr. Jack Zenger and Dr. Joseph Folkman. For many decades, they have researched leadership extensively. In particular, they have always been intrigued by the timeless question of female leadership. Why are there so few women leaders compared to men? Does gender make a difference in the way people lead? Their latest research released in 2019 highlights the following conclusion:

> *"From our analysis... women in leadership positions were perceived as being every bit as effective as men. In fact, while the differences were not huge, women scored at a statistically significantly higher level than men on the vast majority of leadership competencies measured."*
> Jack Zenger and Joseph Folkman

The research is based on 360-degree reviews involving thousands of men and women leaders in some of the most successful and progressive organizations in the world, both public and private, government and commercial, domestic and international. Respondents were asked to rate each leader's effectiveness overall and on 19 competencies that are most important to overall leadership effectiveness.

They found that women are assessed by their managers – particularly male managers – to be slightly more effective than men at every hierarchical level and in virtually every function including the traditional male bastions of IT, operations and legal. They are thought to be more effective in 84% of the 19 competencies.

Capability	Women's percentile	Men's percentile
Takes initiative	55.6	48.2
Resilience	54.7	49.3
Practices self-development	54.8	49.8
Drive for results	53.9	48.8
Displays high integrity and honesty	54.0	49.1
Develops others	54.1	49.8
Inspires and motivates others	53.9	49.7
Bold leadership	53.2	49.8
Builds relationships	53.2	49.9
Champions change	53.1	49.8
Establishes stretch goals	52.6	49.7
Collaboration and teamwork	52.6	50.2
Connects to the outside world	51.6	50.3
Communicates powerfully and prolifically	51.8	50.7
Solves problems and analyzes issues	51.5	50.4
Leadership speed	51.4	50.4
Innovates	51.4	51.0
Technical or professional expertise	50.1	51.1
Develops strategic perspective	50.1	51.4

Note: The T-values of all data are statistically significant
Source: Zenger Folkman 2019

In particular, women were rated as excelling in taking initiative, exhibiting resilience, practicing self-development, driving for results, displaying high integrity and honesty, and developing others. Men on the other hand were rated as being better in two capabilities: developing strategic perspective, and technical or professional expertise.

Women make highly competent leaders, according to people who work very closely with them. What is holding them back is not lack of capability but a dearth of opportunity. When given these opportunities, women are as likely to succeed in higher-level positions as men.

Research 2: Adding women to the C-suite changes how companies think. Researchers at three universities – Lehigh, Maastricht and Antwerp – examined the impact of women on senior management teams. Previously, there had been studies that showed that firms with more senior women leaders are more profitable, more socially responsible, and provide safer, higher-quality customer experiences, among other benefits. But data to explain why having more female executives is associated with better business outcomes has been limited. And what specific mechanisms cause these positive outcomes?

In their research, the researchers focused on 163 multinational companies in the OECD (Organization for Economic Co-operation and Development), located in Europe, the United States and Japan, over 13 years. They have found that firms became more open to change and less risk-seeking after women joined the C-suite; and shifted focus from M&A to internal R&D. The researchers suggest that adding women to the C-suite does not simply bring new perspectives to the top management team, it shifts how top management thinks.

The cognitive shifts with respect to change orientation and greater aversion to risk may be due to the values that women leaders bring. To advance to the highest corporate levels, women have become adept at balancing themselves while walking a tightrope. Hence while standing out by promoting novel strategies, they will carefully weigh their benefits against the risks of potential failure. Over time, as these women executives win the respect and support of their male colleagues, their mindset rubs off on the top management team.

M&A is a *knowledge-buying* strategy which may be described as an aggressive and masculine approach. It may offer a quick win but carries with it inherent risks. This contrasts with R&D, a *knowledge-building* strategy, a more traditionally feminine collaborative approach. It is a carefully calibrated approach requiring patience but carries less risks. Again, through the influence of women leaders, the firms substantially increased their R&D investment and scaled back on M&A.

The researchers found the greatest impact when female executives joined a top management team that already included at least one woman, and when women joined as part of a smaller cohort of new appointees. Taken together, their findings reveal that female top management team appointees contribute to reshaping innovation-oriented renewal strategies in multinational corporations in the span of just a couple of years.

Unlocking gender equality at the workplace

As we enter the third decade of the 21st century, science and technology will continue to blaze new trails. Unfortunately our collective wisdom hasn't evolved fast enough to provide moral, ethical and philosophical guardrails for harnessing our technological prowess. Isaac Asimov, the Russian-born American biochemist and writer once said, "The saddest aspect of life right now is that science gathers knowledge faster than society gathers wisdom."

Many daunting global issues confront mankind. We have not been successful in tackling the calamitous impact of climate change, spread of diseases, racial inequality, poverty, famine, and so on. The leaders who are calling the shots in these areas are almost all males. While they shoulder such responsibilities steadfastly, the other half of humanity – the females – have been denied the opportunity to participate and make a difference. Imagine how society will benefit when women become equal partners in leadership and decision-making in all spheres of human activity.

Ancient sages like Laozi taught us the notion of *yin* and *yang*. *Yin* is associated with the female principle in nature, *yang* with the male. These two forces coexist permanently, complementing each other and creating a continuous virtuous cycle of change. One cannot exist without the other. For far too long, leadership has been defined as the exclusive preserve of men. The time has come for men to recognize that they have much to learn from women on how to lead. It takes humility and wisdom to acknowledge that women are equally suitable for leadership in all sectors as men. When leadership embraces both the feminine and masculine characteristics of humanity, it will be a kinder, safer, wiser and more sustainable world for the generations to come.

Many women are now standing up and claiming their rightful place as leaders. What is holding them back is the barrage of stereotypes, biases and prejudices that they continue to face. Men who currently hold all the cards in organizations are faced with a momentous choice: continue to deny women their place as leaders at the highest levels, or exhibit wisdom and lead the much-needed change. If you are a male leader in the highest echelons of your organization, what actions will you take? If you are a woman leader or aspiring to be a woman leader, what steps can you initiate on your own? How will you plough your own furrow?

20

ARE YOU READY FOR A LARGER ROLE?

It boils down to upgrading your internal OS (operating system)

"We can't solve problems by using the same kind of thinking we used when we created them."
Albert Einstein

Leadership effectiveness is often the number one priority for CEOs. To ensure that they have the quality and quantity of leaders to drive their strategies and grow their business, most companies are investing heavily in developing a talent pipeline. But a paradox soon arises. Though high-potential leaders may be talented, great with people, outstanding in delivery of results and even visionary, when they assume higher responsibilities some may be stymied by the new challenges.

Such leaders can't scale due to their inability to switch their mindset. The higher they go, the greater will be the uncertainty and complexity in their operating environment. And a key requirement is to comprehend the changing environment and in turn communicate it to others as a springboard for change. Without this ability, the people around them will be treading water while the world zooms past them. The two following cases, involving founders of companies, illustrate this dilemma.

Forever 21: The fast-fashion icon that lost its way

Forever 21 was once the world's fastest-growing fast-fashion retailer. In 1981, Korean couple Do Won and Jin Sook Chang immigrated to the US with not much more than a high school education. To make ends meet, they held down numerous gigs. One day it dawned upon the Changs that the people who drove the nicest cars were all in the garment business. Three years later, with $11,000 in savings, they opened their first clothing store in Los Angeles.

Forever 21 was built on the idea that 21 is "the most enviable age." They pioneered the fast-fashion model: identify apparel trends and bring these products to the "trendy, fresh and young in spirit" at low prices. And the concept caught fire immediately. Forever 21 was not only the first, they were also the fastest.

New stores were opened every six months. Even though their products were mass-produced, they were still unique as their stores only sold select styles for a limited time. Soon they were competing directly with iconic global fashion brands like Zara, H&M and Uniqlo. At its peak, the retailer brought in more than $4B in sales from more than 790 stores across 48 countries, operated by more than 43,000 employees. In 2015, the Changs became one of America's wealthiest couples, with a combined net worth of nearly $6B.

In 2016, the tide turned against them like a tsunami. Unable to stanch mounting losses, Forever 21 filed for Chapter 11 bankruptcy protection in September 2019. These were the key factors that sank the once-unstoppable fast-fashion icon:

- Insular and secretive management style – the Changs made all decisions and distrusted outsiders
- Failure to adapt to threats from more agile and digital-first retailers
- Lost sight of their customers, resulting in a disastrous merchandizing strategy
- Disruption by the ferocious pace of e-commerce and digitalization

- Stumped by the complexity of globalization
- Obsession with brick-and-mortar stores

In short, as the business grew rapidly, the founders stayed trapped in a mindset more suited for a start-up in the 1980s. They floundered because they had not upgraded their thinking and capabilities.

Dell: The transformation journey from PCs to IT powerhouse

In 1984, Michael Dell, a 19-year-old student, launched his business in his dorm room at the University of Texas with only $1,000. He had an idea to provide affordable personal computers to college students. By bypassing the indirect retail channel, he made PCs much more affordable and earned high profits for himself. Another benefit was that customers could personalize the features they preferred. He then developed a manufacturing process to mass produce made-to-order units. Such innovations led to a revolution in the IT industry.

Dell has led his eponymous company for the last 36 years through an evolutionary journey, transforming its business model many times along the way. Today, Dell Technologies (as it is now called) has become a $90B-a-year technology powerhouse. It has a stake in storage, servers, data protection and networking along with its hardware products like monitors, printers and, of course, PCs. These are key building blocks to deliver multi-cloud and hybrid cloud solutions.

What has made Michael Dell the transformational leader he is? Industry insiders say that he has demonstrated time and again the ability to upgrade his mindset, embrace risk like a start-up and learn quickly from mistakes. He started out as a PC hobbyist and has always been geeky. Over time, his perspective has grown in multiple dimensions. From a device-centric view, he has embraced a more systems orientation.

He frequently advises small business owners to determine their optimal point of impact. What are the few critical things you should focus on to take your organization forward as you expand? "When I had a small number of people, I was doing everything myself," he said. "But now that I have thousands, I am completely focused on strategy." He also reminds executives and entrepreneurs to surround themselves with the best people. These smart people will challenge the organizations and force them to think differently.

Upgrade your internal OS

As leaders move up the organization, they need to transform their mindset. Our mindset is our internal OS (operating system). Much as in a computer, the OS is in the background all the time. It is all-seeing and all-knowing. And it dictates everything that leaders do – mostly unconsciously. If a leader's OS is not upgraded continually, he will not be equal to the rising complexity of his role. Simply adding more apps won't be the solution.

To be sure, apps such as decision-making, critical thinking, data analytics, constructive conflict resolution, delegation and coaching, building high performance teams and so on, are all important competencies for leaders. But for these to be put into use, leaders must first evolve to higher-order thinking and being. Otherwise, more apps will jam up their OS and lead to a crash.

High-performing leaders are alike in their ability to deliver great business results. But they are different in a crucial way. Some can scale while others can't. The key determinant lies with their internal operating system. Leaders who are able to scale, i.e. prepare themselves for higher office, need to develop themselves horizontally as well as vertically.

- **Horizontal development** refers to acquiring more skills and competencies. It is about what you know and how you can achieve your goals. People who do this exceedingly well are called high-performing leaders. For instance, in this digital era, we have to learn how to lead differently and not cling onto outmoded styles of leadership. Though we need not be experts in the new ABCs (AI, Big Data and Cloud), we'll need to develop passion for digital technology.

- **Vertical development** refers to continually upgrading your sense-making capability. From a developmental perspective, it means a qualitative shift in the way of thinking. Otherwise you can't make meaning and provide guidance in a climate of increasing complexity and ambiguity. The key is to grow. We grow when our understanding changes; we often call it "transformation."

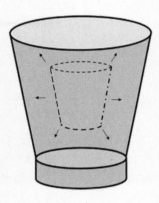

The illustration above shows graphically the difference between horizontal and vertical development. In horizontal development, the leaders keep adding more leadership knowledge in a cup that is already full. They will leverage such skills and knowledge to move towards their goals. The limiting factor is not the content; it is the cup (the leader's mind). In vertical development the aim is not to add more to the cup but to grow the size of the cup itself. If horizontal development is about *transferring information* to the leader, vertical development is about the *transformation* of the leader.

Let's be clear. Traditional, horizontal competencies still matter. But for the leaders who aspire to lead at enterprise level, they will need to transform their sense-making ability. Economist and complexity thinker Brian Arthur uses a gambling analogy to illustrate the profound ambiguity and uncertainty that leaders face in the digital world that necessitates a great need for sense-making.

Imagine you are in a large casino with many top leaders of the business space you are in. At one table, there is a game called Blockchain. Over at another, there is a game called Augmented Reality. As you look around, you notice people heading towards other tables offering Cloud Technologies and IOT (Internet of Things). Your interest is piqued.

You sit at one table and ask, "How much to play?"

"$1.5 billion," the croupier replies.

"Who'll be playing?"

"We don't know yet. They'll soon be showing up."

"What are the rules? What are the odds of winning?" you ask nervously.

"We can't say for sure. Do you still want to play?"

As you're now a senior leader in your organization, you don't really have a choice to play or not. All companies will become digitalized. You will need some degree of technical expertise, deep pockets, will, luck and courage. Above all, the rewards go to the players who are first to make sense of the new games looming out of the technological fog, to recognize them and seize the opportunity.

Sense-making at Eisai Co.

Eisai Co., Ltd is a Japanese pharmaceutical company headquartered in Tokyo, Japan. It has some 10,000 employees, among them about 1,500 in research. Eisai is known for having developed medicines to treat dementia. As with many pharma companies, the focus was completely on the development of drugs. How they will impact the needs of the patients and their families was secondary. Haruo Naito, Eisai's president, saw the need to make a major mindset shift to embrace the company's mission of human health care. He sent all their researchers to interact with patients at hospitals. They learned how patients behave, take medications, bathe, and communicate with caregivers. One researcher said, "I was completely focused on the development of medicines, but at the hospital the focus was not on medicines. Drugs are only useful in certain situations. The training gave me fresh awareness of the purpose of the drugs and how we should develop them."

Leadership altitudes

Ram Charan, renowned business advisor and author, takes this concept of mindset shifts further when he develops the notion of leadership altitudes. He postulates three critical leadership altitudes: 50,000 feet, 50 feet and 5 feet. Leaders who are able to scale can navigate with ease, and make connections, between all three altitudes. Mountaineers who successfully guide their teams up the most challenging and treacherous slopes all have an internal OS with such versatility.

At 50,000 feet, leaders see higher and further. They take in the big picture and make meaning from the confusing and contradictory signals in the environment. From this they will share their insights and intuition with their teams on how to lead changes to better serve their customers, markets and communities.

At 50 feet, leaders and their teams develop concrete action plans to drive their short- and medium-term goals. Execution will be key. No company can stay healthy if this is not done well consistently. To this end, leaders will surround themselves with the best people, and champion the development of people at all levels. Everyone accomplishes more in a culture of openness, collaboration and interdependence.

At 5 feet, leaders pause regularly to introspect about themselves. First to examine their strengths and liabilities. Second to draw lessons from daily experiences. What is their inner life telling them? What behaviors are they manifesting, consciously as well as unconsciously? What must they do to be more congruent across all three altitudes? What are the various perspectives about challenges, some of which are polar opposites? Is it time for another OS upgrade?

Here are some differences between leaders who have upgraded their mindset compared to those who are still stuck in an outmoded mindset.

Outmoded mindset	Upgraded OS
A single unchanging worldview	Multiple, continually evolving worldviews
Focus on functional KPIs	Focus on shared purpose
Success is due to individuals	Success is due to teams
Conflict is the clash of us vs them	Conflict may be due to multiple factors
Always busy and on the go	Pause, reflect and learn
Either-or	Both-and
Ask "Why?"	Ask "Why not?"
Struggling with ambiguity and changes	Comfortable with uncertainty and lack of data
Left-brained	Left- and right-brained
Results first	Results, people and the larger good
Sees separate parts of the situation	Sees interconnecting patterns and connections

21

SEEKING YOUR TRUE SELF

Your future self will be different from your current self

"Human beings are works in progress that mistakenly think they're finished."
Daniel Gilbert, Harvard psychologist

A few years ago, Salma, a business leader, received her 360-degree feedback report, an exercise that is administered for top management in her company. During the debrief discussions, one aspect of the report stood out. Nearly all respondents highlighted as her key strength her ability to be candid and direct in expressing her opinions, whether it be at meetings or in one-on-one conversations. As one respondent put it, "Salma does not agree for the sake of harmony. She will speak up openly and forcefully if she thinks otherwise. I wish all leaders had her courage."

There were, however, also comments that ran counter to these such as, "As Salma is very confident and forceful, it is difficult for her to accept opinions that are contrary to her perspective." Throughout the report, respondents at all levels of direct reports, peers and even bosses, sprinkled similar comments on both sides of the divide. Then in the quantitative ratings section, she scored the highest on "Showing confidence" and "Speaking up about problems." Her lowest scores were on "Openness to diverse ideas" and "Being approachable."

This was the second time that such a 360-degree feedback was administered. The first was three years ago, when Salma was in a lower position. After studying the report, she said, "I'm glad that people acknowledge my consistency. I'm not about to change as I wish to remain authentic as a leader."

Now consider James, a newly appointed manager in a tech company in Sydney. He is a tall and imposing figure with a booming voice to match. People who attend the same meetings with him for the first time often sense a disconnect between what they see and what they hear. James prefers to listen thoughtfully to others rather than to jump into a robust exchange of views. He tends to be soft-spoken and values decision-making by consensus.

One day, James's manager meets with him for a casual chat over coffee. Her feedback is rather indirect and nuanced, but the gist that James gathers is that he has to figure out how he wishes to show up as a leader. Otherwise, in the Australian culture where people speak quite freely, he may be overshadowed. And how will others know what is on his mind if he keeps his views to himself?

This is not the first time that James has received such inputs. That has always been him – deliberate, thoughtful and considerate. He is no pushover, though. When he feels strongly about something, he will speak up. But clearly, his boss thinks he needs to do it more readily and frequently. This does give him some discomfort. How should he step up without behaving like a fake?

Human beings are works in progress

In two decades of work on leadership development with leaders at various levels, I frequently encounter the dilemmas that Salma and James have found themselves in. It centers around the need to be authentic – being true to yourself. In one of Shakespeare's most famous plays, *Hamlet*, Polonius gives this advice to his son, Laertes, who is about to embark for school in France, "This above all: to thine own self be true." The conventional interpretation is that Laertes should behave consistently with his personal values. Otherwise he'll come across as disingenuous and lacking in integrity.

This is sound fatherly advice. But it has also given rise to the timeless debate on authenticity and the dilemmas that people have faced regarding what their true self is. It is important for us all to pause and consider the concept of self.

The father in *Hamlet* implies that his young son already has a "self" that is well-developed and stable. How realistic is this? In our modern age, there are two factors that may militate against this supposition. First, in the course of our life journey, we are constantly growing and evolving. Hence, as we acquire more knowledge, experience and wisdom, our sense of self will gradually but surely change. Secondly, the world around us is complex and changing constantly. How do we adapt if we insist that our sense of self must remain unwavering?

In his TED talk, "The Psychology of Your Future Self," Harvard psychologist Dr. Daniel Gilbert explains that nearly all of us are affected by an illusion that our present self is the "real" and "finished" version of ourselves, and our future self will be basically the same as who we are today. Citing a recently published study that spans more than 60 years, Gilbert and his co-workers discovered that personalities, skills, likes and dislikes change over time. It involved thousands of people of various groups ranging from 18 to 68 years old. They asked half of them to predict how much their values would change in the next 10 years, and the other half to tell how much their values had changed in the last 10 years. This enabled them to compare the predictions of people, say, 18 years old, to the reports of people who were 28 years old, and to do that kind of analysis throughout the lifespan. This what they found.

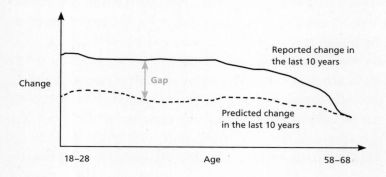

174

In all areas such as personalities, values, likes and dislikes and so on, there are substantial changes as people age. The gap shows the difference. While the change slows down as we age, at every age people underestimate how much their personalities will change in the next decade. Our future self will be significantly different from our current self.

Let's now look deeper into a set of data that will shed light on how our work style varies with age.

How management style varies with age

A 2019 study of managers by the *MIT Sloan Management Review* is a real eye-opener. The five researchers led by Julian Birkinshaw of London Business School surveyed 10,000 managers between ages 21 and 70 working in multiple industries and in 20 countries. What they found is that younger and older managers have different perspectives about how to lead others. They concluded that management style varies more with age than any other characteristic in the study. The style differences are most significant in five critical areas:

- **Managing external context:** This means everything outside the boundaries of the organization, including developing an understanding of the operating environment, thinking strategically, and learning to work with external stakeholders. They found that older managers put greater emphasis on core competencies, customer relationships, and other big-picture factors central to a company's identity, while younger managers are more focused on the company's positioning in its competitive marketplace.

- **Managing internal context:** This refers to the way people get things done in an organization, including managing vertically and horizontally, communication and leading change. Younger managers are more self-centric and look for ways to build value for themselves such as finding a good mentor, asking for feedback, asserting themselves, and getting recognition. Older managers are more oriented towards collaboration: building rapport, building networks for support, and anticipating problems and concerns.

- **Managing people:** The most effective managers are those that provide the conditions that enable their people to be successful. This includes developing others through motivation, delegation and providing feedback. Older managers tend to favor more personalized approaches such as listening carefully, developing empathy and providing effective feedback. Younger managers gravitate towards technical approaches such as problem-solving. They favor hard skills until such time they discover that soft skills are crucial to their success.

- **Managing tasks:** In terms of problem-solving and decision-making, all respondents recognized that bringing people together to solve problems is important. But older manager value this more than younger managers. In contrast, younger managers prioritize structured techniques like analyzing a process for possible points of failure more than older managers.

- **Managing yourself:** All respondents support the view that understanding oneself is essential to becoming an effective manager. But they focus on different aspects. Older managers feel that it is important to be aware of how your actions impact others in order to build resilience and recover from setbacks. Younger managers say demonstrating initiative is more important.

As we compare the differences in management styles, we can look at them through the lens of increasing personal maturity. This suggests that managers in their 20s and 30s are on a journey of personal discovery, learning through trial and error and self-analysis. As they become older and more experienced, they understand themselves better, and a more mature and wiser sense of self will have evolved.

What then is our true self?

In *Hamlet* when young Laertes is advised by his father to embark on his learning journey with a clear sense of who he is, it may turn out to be a prescription for a fixed mindset instead of a growth mindset (see Chapter 10). Your "true self" is not fixed and static. It can and should evolve with experience, discovering new facets of yourself as you move on to bigger and more complex responsibilities.

Illustrative of this is the conundrum faced by young people who are about to embark on their university education. What career do they wish to pursue? This will determine the courses they enroll in. Is it economics, medicine, architecture, engineering, liberal arts? Many young people think they know their calling. And so confidently they choose their disciplines in their freshman year, no doubt with a little boost from their parents. In their sophomore year, they may find out that that's not what interests them. In some cases, after graduation, they may even decide to pursue a career completely different from their studies. Is this fickleness? Perhaps not. We don't really know sufficiently what path we should pursue in the early years of our life.

Let's circle back to Salma and James whom we met at the beginning. Salma sees herself as a courageous leader who speaks truth to power and all others. She has built a reputation for this and it has served her well so far. Thus despite its downsides, she is unwilling to moderate her style. Six months later, the company's employee engagement report is published. Now this is a wakeup call for her. On a number of scales, her scores are the lowest among all peers. The overarching feedback is that she has overplayed her hand in being outspoken. Her blind side: she is so intent on having the last say that she shuts others down.

Chastened, Salma decides to request for executive coaching support. Through the coaching dialogues, she takes on a new perspective. She learns to be less self-centered and to appreciate the impact of her behaviors on others around her. As a first step, she realizes that it is not the "what" but the "how" that needs modification. She does not need to stop speaking up. That is her strength. What she does need to do is to take a more balanced approach between advocacy and listening with curiosity and empathy. Asking open-ended questions will be a skill to hone.

This is a defining moment for Salma. Her narrative is no longer about the lone individual who speaks out fearlessly in a rather contentious environment. As a senior leader, she needs to get past this. It is now about how she demonstrates her ability to look beyond herself to the people who see her as a leader. In this instance, how can she speak up courageously and create a psychologically safe environment for people to feel that their opinions are valued?

As for James, after the initial chat with his boss, he decides to approach her for more counsel. He quickly realizes that emotionally he has not stepped up to his new role as a manager. In his mind, he is still burdened by the fact that his new peers were, only a short while back, one level higher than him in the organization. Being the new kid on the block, he hesitates to be more forthcoming until he has found his footing.

But gaining respect and credibility from fellow managers must be done in parallel with behaving like a manager now. Waiting until he is fully settled in is not an option. Though his private sense of self is that of a thoughtful and quiet individual who speaks only when he needs to, "how he shows up" as his boss put it, is now a key success factor. Furthermore, he does not need to feel like a fake as he does have useful ideas and opinions to share. James is now committed to stepping out of his comfort zone and experimenting with new ways of communicating with others.

In praise of the incomplete self

We are all works in progress. Our sense of self will continue to evolve as we become more experienced, older and wiser. The stories that we hold in our head about who we are can become obsolete as we progress. We must therefore be willing to revise these narratives and edit them in the years ahead. This is related to the forging of a personal leadership brand, i.e. what do we wish to be known for and how do we add value to the people we serve. By adapting and trying new behaviors that make us uncomfortable, our future self will be a better version of our current self.

22

CULTIVATING THE UNEXPECTED

**Success happens at the intersection
of talent, hard work and luck**

*"Luck is very important. Of course you can't wait for luck,
because it won't come. While you start a journey, luck
may eventually come to you."*
Jack Ma

When a friend of mine first started out after graduation as a research scientist in a university, his manager said this to him, "To be successful in science, you need two out of three things: smart, hard work and luck. Since you are probably smart and cannot control luck, you'd better work really hard." This really was sound advice, and he took it to heart.

It has been more than 20 years, and my friend changed a few companies since then. When we met up recently, he was president of a well-known pharmaceutical company. We looked back at the valuable tip that he had received fresh out of school. This is what he said, "I shall always be grateful to my first boss for starting me off on the right footing. Ability and hard work are foundational stones. Without these two, nothing meaningful and sustainable will come about. But I have also learned that the role of luck in our success is far greater than we realize."

We all have no trouble acknowledging that there is no substitute for talent and hard work. But luck? How can any level-headed person count on something as capricious and unpredictable as luck? But haven't we met smart and hard-working friends or colleagues who seem to be at a dead end? And there are some people who just have the knack of getting whatever they set their minds to? Is it luck? If so, why do some people have it more than others? As we'll find out shortly, luck isn't entirely luck.

A scientific study on luck

Richard J. Wiseman is the head of a psychology research department at the University of Hertfordshire. For over ten years, he and his colleagues at the university's Perrott-Warrick Research Unit examined the behaviors of over 1,000 volunteers who considered themselves "lucky" or "unlucky," conducting thousands of interviews and hundreds of experiments. Wiseman's findings resulted in a radical new way of looking at luck.

Here is a glimpse of what Wiseman uncovered in his lab. He gave people a newspaper and asked them to count the number of photographs inside. It was a rather trivial task. Everybody would go through the process, and after about three pages, there was a massive half-page advert saying, "STOP COUNTING. THERE ARE 43 PHOTOGRAPHS IN THIS NEWSPAPER." It was next to a photo, so participants were looking in that area. A few pages later, there was another massive advert that said, "STOP COUNTING. TELL THE EXPERIMENTER YOU'VE SEEN THIS AD AND WIN £150." Self-professed unlucky people took about two minutes to count the 43 photographs. They missed all the ads that were literally shouting in their faces. Lucky people took seconds as they spotted the messages right away.

The element of luck in scientific discoveries

Alexander Fleming is credited with the discovery of penicillin in 1928. At that time, he was experimenting with the influenza virus in a laboratory at St. Mary's Hospital in London. Often described as a careless researcher, he returned from a two-week vacation to find that a mold had developed on an accidentally contaminated staphylococcus culture plate. Upon examination, he noticed that the culture prevented the growth of staphylococci. He discerned that it was not the mold itself but some "juice" it had produced that had killed the bacteria. He isolated the culture and named it penicillin. Later, he would say: "When I woke up just after dawn on September 28, 1928, I certainly didn't plan to revolutionize all medicine by discovering the world's first antibiotic, or bacteria killer. But I suppose that was exactly what I did."

While there are many great scientific discoveries that came only after years, even decades, of goal-oriented work, Fleming's happened by accident. There are many other incredible breakthroughs in the world that came about when someone found something that they weren't looking for. They have changed our lives for the better. Examples: microwave ovens, quinine, X-rays, radioactivity, Velcro, Viagra, insulin, and so on.

As the foregoing examples show, unexpected things turn up all the time. In fact, scientists are acknowledging that it's how science happens. There is now serious research in the emerging field of serendipity. The 18th-century British writer Horace Walpole was captivated by a Persian fable about three princes from the Isle of Serendip. He wrote to a friend suggesting that this old tale contained a crucial idea about human genius. Walpole said, "As their highnesses travelled, they were always making discoveries, by accident and sagacity, of things which they were not in quest of." He then coined a new word *serendipity*, defining it as "that quality of mind which, through awareness, sagacity, and good fortune, allows one to frequently discover something good while seeking something else." Even at its birth, serendipity meant a skill rather than a random stroke of good fortune.

> *"Serendipity is the quality of mind which, through awareness, sagacity, and good fortune, allows one to frequently discover something good while seeking something else."*
> Horace Walpole

Before we turn to the practical question of how we may cultivate serendipity for the greater fulfilment of our lives, let's dip quickly into this fairy tale that so inspired Walpole.

The three princes of Serendip

The story is set in the fifth century AD in the royal days of Anuradhapura on the island of Ceylon, now called Sri Lanka. It was then known as Serendip. The original fable was passed from one generation to the next and there are several different versions. All are essentially about the gift of finding valuable or agreeable things not sought after originally.

King Jafer had three sons. This wise and powerful king wanted to prepare his sons well so that someday they could become good rulers. There were three fields that he wished for them to master: virtue, science and wisdom. And so, the wise king assigned wiser men and women to teach his sons. These teachers imparted not only knowledge but moral lessons, and showed the boys to see and perceive with both their eyes and their hearts.

As the three princes grew older, the king decided to test them one at a time. He said to each prince that he would like him to be the new king, holding the crown over the boy's head. The first prince noticed that his father was holding onto the crown very tightly, and he replied that he was not ready for the throne. The second and third sons similarly declined. King Jafer was pleased. Each of his sons had acquired wisdom and humility.

To complete their education, King Jafer decided to send his sons to other lands. Only then would they get to know about other people in the world, be exposed to new ideas, and understand the diverse ways of thinking, of living, and of being. The three princes, travelling incognito and wearing plain clothing, set off on their journey. In the years ahead, they encountered numerous challenges. Many of these were life-threatening to the inhabitants of the land they visited. In every case, they willingly undertook to help the distressed people. They would speak with them, asking questions politely and respectfully, and listening deeply. People were naturally inclined to like and help them. Through this approach, they learned much and were able to resolve problems to everyone's satisfaction.

One particular incident is worthy of further discussion. One day,

THE WAY OF THE LEADER

they passed a camel owner whose camel had run away. The man asked whether they had seen a wandering camel. The princes said no. They then asked some questions. Did the camel have only one eye? Was it missing a tooth? Was it limping? Was the camel carrying butter and honey? The answers to these were all affirmative. Now the camel owner became convinced that the young men had stolen his camel, had them arrested and brought to court. Subsequently, the camel owner burst into the courtroom, saying that he had found the camel and begged for forgiveness for falsely accusing the three princes.

How did the three brothers know so much about the camel they had never seen? It was through their power of observation. The grass was nibbled on only one side of the road, so they knew that the camel had lost an eye. They noticed partly chewed bits of grass, and concluded that they had dropped though the gap of a missing tooth. And in the tracks themselves, they saw evidence of a dragging rear leg. As for butter and honey? The brothers noticed ants, which sought after fat on the left side of the road, and flies, which sought after sweet on the right.

How can we harness the unexpected?

How would we have fared if we were put in the same spot as the three princes? In the lab test on counting photographs conducted by Wisemen, people didn't even see what was in plain sight. And many scientists and inventors had to trip over the truth before they could see it. As mentioned elsewhere in this book, many business leaders willfully ignored signs of changing consumer demands and sent their companies into a death spiral.

As we see every day in all walks of life, events are happening around us. What matters most is whether we notice these happenings and what we do with them. One scientist, Dr. Sanda Erdelez, who studies serendipity, says that people fall into four distinct groups: non-encounterers, occasional encounterers, encounterers and super-encounterers. Non-encounters are the constantly busy type who stick to their To Do list or a prescribed process when doing a piece of work. They have a narrow vision, like race horses with blinkers on. When searching for information, they don't wander off into the margins. The occasional encounterers stumble into new bits of information once in a while but don't see their relevance to what they are looking for. Encounterers do recognize interesting information that appears but treat it as a chance event. Most interesting are the super-encounterers. Like Wiseman's lucky people, they habitually encounter new and interesting insights every way they look. They have developed an addiction to prospecting and will happily spend countless hours looking in some of the oddest places because they expect to find treasures there.

Here are a few steps that you may take to increase your chances of discovering your lucky breaks.

1. Be curious: Throughout the day, many things are happening around us. Lucky people are on the lookout for events or happenings that just suddenly happen. By consciously adopting a curious approach towards life, they tend to notice more of their surroundings. When these happen, they are able to see connections between seemingly unrelated events or experiences. But these may not quite make sense at first blush. Hashing it out with friends and co-workers may lift the veil though. Knowing that you don't know and seeking other people's perspectives is sagacious.

It also helps to read widely, going beyond what is relevant to one's occupation. Explore new experiences and fields far removed from day-to-day relevance. Building and maintaining a strong network of friends is useful. Bring something interesting to this network to keep it real and vibrant.

For example, a few years ago, while driving along Orchard Road in the heart of Singapore's central business district, I saw someone I knew from Paris waiting at the traffic junction. This was unexpected. A few minutes later, I searched for her contact on LinkedIn and emailed her. It turned out that she was here on a visit to her new company, a French fashion and luxury goods company. A few months later, I was invited to work with the company on a multi-year project.

"If you open your eyes, you will see things worth seeing."
Rumi, Sufi mystic and poet

2. Be an artist: We are all trained to be wary of going by gut feel. This is good advice that we should be mindful of. However, if we are going to base all decisions and actions on hard data, it will severely hamper us from acting spontaneously. Essentially what it means is that we are relying exclusively on our left brain. The human brain consists of two hemispheres. The left brain is often described as logical, sequential and literal. Its strengths are in language, critical thinking, numbers, reasoning and analysis. The right brain is better at expressive and creative activities. Its strong suits are inventiveness, empathy, emotional connection, intuitiveness, images, playfulness, music and big-picture thinking. In the digital age, AI will soon take over all the logical activities. We need not feel threatened though. We can collaborate with AI by tapping into our humanity. By seeing the world through the eyes of artists, we combine substance with style, fun and originality.

3. Stay optimistic: Have you ever made a prediction about your life that came true? Were you surprised that you can sometimes be surprisingly accurate in your predictions? For instance, you might predict that a project you and your team members are working on will turn out exceedingly well. The other members all feel the same way. And true enough, nine months later, all your collaboration pays off and senior management compliments the team for a job well done. Alternatively, you were nervous about a speech you had to give at a work event in the afternoon. You spent the whole morning rehearsing the presentation again and again. At that event, you were all jitters and could not remember the flow of your message when speaking.

Both of these are examples of a well-known psychological phenomenon called self-fulfilling prophecies. Unconsciously, our expectations will influence our behavior. Therefore it is important to cultivate a sense of optimism and to believe in yourself. Of course, effort and preparation must first precede the event. Once that is done, stop worrying. Just relax and trust yourself.

4. Reflect, draw lessons, and act: This is what Jack Ma meant. Act decisively when Lady Luck smiles on you. She seldom knocks twice. Bill Gates adds, "I was lucky to be in the right place at the right time. But many others were also in the same place. The difference was that I took action."

23

IN PRAISE OF THE INDIRECT APPROACH

Why objectives are often best pursued indirectly

"He who knows of the direct and indirect approaches will be victorious."
Sunzi, Chinese military strategist

The Art of War attributed to Sunzi (or Sun Tzu) is one of the world's most influential books on military strategy. Written 2,500 years ago in China, it is now studied in military academies around the globe. Indeed, General David Petraeus, former Director of the CIA (Central Intelligence Agency), reaffirmed its relevance in the 21st century. Its teachings are useful not only in the battlefield but also in work and life in general.

Sunzi advises repeatedly that the best strategy is the one that delivers victory without fighting. Of course, this is not always possible. But choosing headlong confrontation as the default mode will result in a protracted campaign that will cost both sides dearly. Therefore, take the indirect approach whenever possible.

In conventional business practice, the preferred approach to managing a project is to be methodical, purposeful and well-organized. This is the direct approach. If you are responsible for building a new shopping mall, or overseeing the implementation of an ERP (enterprise resource planning) system or software for your company, it will involve many parties, partners and vendors. A lot of upfront planning is absolutely necessary. All important aspects need to be well-defined and time-lined even before the project commences. But what if you are now launching a massive cultural change program? If you are leading a start-up with three college friends with the aim of gaining a foothold in a market space dominated by established players, would you adopt the direct approach?

The direct approach to problem-solving works best if you have complete understanding of your objectives, and the environment that you operate in is stable, predictable and within your control. With one-dimensional and transparent objectives, it is possible to determine when and whether the goals have been achieved. Such is the case with building a new shopping mall in an urban district.

However, if the operating environment is unstable, unpredictable and complex, and your knowledge is necessarily fragmented and imperfect, then your objectives are generally best accomplished indirectly rather than directly. This is the challenge faced by a start-up planning to launch an attack in a market space dominated by powerful competitors.

Crossing the streets of Ho Chi Minh City provides an apt metaphor for taking the indirect approach. Once, standing at the kerb-side, watching in bewilderment as a swarm of scooters, motorcycles and cars zipped by, I was given a tip by a friendly shopkeeper, "Walk slowly. Stay calm. The motorists will avoid you." I did so with trepidation, and survived. Paraphrasing Sunzi, "When there is confusion around you, don't be petrified. Take the first step cautiously, and learn as you go along."

Let's now explore how the indirect approach is applied in some real-life situations.

How Apple and Google took an indirect approach against Microsoft

In 2000, Microsoft owned the entire OS market for all computer devices – desktop and laptop PCs. With their 100% domination, any would-be challenger knew that it would be committing hara-kiri to compete head-on with this juggernaut. At that time, the number one maker of mobile phones was Research in Motion, which owned BlackBerry. They imploded suddenly as Apple's iPhone quickly overwhelmed them. A small upstart by the name of Google was taking its first breath. It began by dabbling in the search engine arena and was a virtual unknown. Google had big dreams, though. They wanted a slice of the OS market. In the meantime, Microsoft was embroiled in an antitrust trial, and didn't think that iPhone was going to amount to anything as it did not have the Windows OS.

This was the market turmoil that Apple and Google found themselves in. Turmoil and opportunity are two sides of the same coin. Both Apple and Google seized it eagerly. As sales of Apple's iPhone started skyrocketing, their iOS soon became the leader in the smartphone OS space. In 2005, Google purchased Android, a start-up in Silicon Valley. Using the skills of their new Android team members, Google developed the Android OS. Google soon launched their Android phones, and leased their open-source Android OS to phone makers such as Samsung, Amazon and Huawei and other Chinese phone makers. This was a stroke of genius that they had picked up from Microsoft in the PC space. Some years later, Google would draw enormous benefits from this against Apple, which kept their iOS closely guarded

According to IDC, in 2020, Google's Android and Apple's iOS have a combined share of 100% of the mobile phone OS market, with Google at 85% and Apple at 15%. This was the outcome of the classic flanking attack by Google and Apple against Microsoft. They knew that they could not do a frontal assault on Microsoft so they chose the mobile phone route. Sales of mobile phones and tablets continue to climb while sales of PCs are declining. As PC sales are cannibalized by mobile phones and tablets, Google and Apple have successfully eroded Microsoft's foothold in the PC OS space.

The entrepreneurial practices of a Chinese restaurant chain

Gao Defu is the owner of Dumpling Xi, a restaurant chain famous for its dumplings which he founded 20 years ago in China. He has more than 500 stores and some 8,000 employees. A few years ago, he noticed that online food delivery services were cannibalizing his in-store sales. He had to quickly digitalize. Fang Ruan, a BCG consultant based in Beijing who shared Gao's story in a TED talk said, "If I were to advise Gao back then, I would go directly with the classical approach, hiring venture managers, providing training on how to integrate online-offline sales, or having some high potentials fully dedicated to the new job, such as a Chief Digital Officer."

To her surprise, Gao adopted a two-hat management system. He invited five successful regional heads to double-hat at headquarters. This meant that they had two roles: lead the drive to develop and implement an online business model, while still being responsible for their brick-and-mortar stores. None of the regional heads had any formal training or related experience in this field. And neither did their boss, Gao. This was certainly unconventional and fraught with risk. When queried, Gao smiled, "This is my dumpling way." Gao's employees were equally perplexed. In the first three months, they ran into difficulties, with sales dropping by 20%. But the boss was unfazed.

The regional heads were quick on the uptick, picking up new skills while still doing their job. Like what kinds of dumpling could be sold online and how to digitalize their supply chain. After the transition, they saw sales picking up. A couple of years later, as revenue continued to grow, new talents were hired. The competencies that had made them nimble and successful are now part of their company's DNA.

Want to help someone? Shut up and listen

Ernesto Sirolli, a noted authority in the field of sustainable economic development, shared a humorous and thought-provoking lesson in a TED talk he gave in 2012. He discussed the unintended consequences of a direct approach in rendering aid to underdeveloped countries.

When Sirolli worked for an Italian NGO (non-governmental organization) on technical cooperation with African countries, he and his colleagues decided to teach Zambian people how to grow food in their first project. They arrived with Italian seeds in southern Zambia and proceeded to impart knowledge to the local people about growing Italian tomatoes and zucchini. They soon found out that the Zambians had absolutely no interest in doing that, so they paid them to come and work. Sometimes, some would turn up. It was amazing to Sirolli and his colleagues that in such a fertile valley next to the Zambezi River, the local people had no plans for agriculture. But instead of asking them how come they weren't growing anything, they simply said, "Thank God we're here. Just in the nick of time to save the Zambian people from starvation."

Everything grew beautifully. The tomatoes were double the size of those in Italy. Soon the Italians were telling the Zambians, "Look how easy agriculture is." One day, when the tomatoes were nice, ripe and red, 200 hippos came out from the river and ate everything up. The Italians exclaimed, "My God, the hippos." And the Zambians replied, "Yes, that's why we have no agriculture here." "Why didn't you tell us?" "You never asked."

It wasn't just the Italians blundering around in Africa. The Americans, English and the French were doing the same. "We Western people are imperialists, colonialist missionaries, and there are only two ways we deal with people: We either patronize them, or we are paternalistic. The two words come from the Latin root *pater*, which means father. But they mean two different things. Paternalistic: I treat anybody from a different culture as if they were my children – 'I love you so much.' Patronizing: I treat everybody from another culture as if they were my servants. That's why the whites in Africa are called *bwana* – boss."

Sirolli was distraught. He thought that they were good people and were doing good work in Africa. Instead, everything they touched they killed. A few years later, he invented a system called Enterprise Facilitation: "You never initiate anything, you never motivate anybody, but you become a servant of local people who have a dream to become a better person. So what do you do? You shut up. You never arrive in a community with any ideas. You sit with the local people. We don't work from offices. We meet at the café. We meet at the pub. We have zero infrastructure. And what we do, we become friends, and we find out what they want to do."

By 2012, Sirolli and his friends had helped 300 communities around the world, and given life to 40,000 businesses. Today, Enterprise Facilitation continues to empower communities to take responsibility for their own economic and community development. It's person-centered rather than program-centered, and bottom-up rather than top-down, a philosophy that is antithetical to the leadership taught in business schools and pursued by the world's largest enterprises.

Why the indirect or oblique approach is best for complex situations

Here are the key reasons:

1. Unknown unknowns. At a news briefing in 2002, the then US Secretary of Defense Donald Rumsfeld explained the limitations of intelligence reports: "There are known knowns. These are things we know we know. We also know there are known unknowns. That is to say, we know there are some things we do not know. But there are also unknown unknowns, the ones we don't know we don't know."

	Known	Unknown
Known	Known Knowns	Known Unknowns
Unknown	Unknown Knowns	Unknown Unknowns

While the remarks initially led to some ridicule towards the Bush administration in general and Rumsfeld in particular, the consensus regarding it has shifted over the years, and it now enjoys some level of respect. Rumsfeld's statements may be mind-bending but his logic is sound. No matter how much we think we know, it pales in comparison to what we don't know. We simply don't know what we don't know.

> *"To know, yet to think that one does not know, is best.*
> *Not to know, yet to think that one knows,*
> *will lead to difficulty."*
> Laozi

Former US president Trump made a bold promise to have 20 million Covid-19 vaccine inoculations of Americans before the end of 2020. By January 2021, however, only 2.8 million people in the US had their jabs. The slow start to the vaccination program was beset by logistical problems and overstretched hospitals. What if there had been bottom-up consultations involving the various stakeholders before setting the 20 million target?

2. Our mental models may not be relevant. There is a saying, "The map is not the territory." We all carry such a map in our head. If the terrain has changed drastically, the map may not be useful. More important will be the contextual knowledge that must accompany the interpretation of the map. Sirolli and company found this out the hard way in Zambia.

In 1979, Sony's co-founder Akio Morita upended the music industry with the Walkman through his new mental model of what music lovers wanted. Decades later, his successors did not update their mental model and hence lost out in the digital music space. Another visionary, Steve Jobs, reinterpreted Morita's idea and invented the iPod.

In the 1990s, a group of developers at Microsoft came up with an innovative device for reading electronic books. This was something that had no precedent as no such product existed as a commercial entity.

The team was excited and they sent the working prototype to Bill Gates, then the CEO. He rapidly rejected the idea. It did not fit in with the Microsoft business strategy and the product did not have the Windows look or feel. Microsoft missed the opportunity. Amazon went on to develop the Kindle, which became a huge business based on e-books. In turning down the e-reader, Gates was displaying a trait common among leaders. He rejected something with an uncertain future and which did not fit into his mental model.

3. We don't know what the right objectives are. With so much fuzziness and uncertainty, we'll have to treat our initial goals as tentative. Only through the process of doing and experimenting can we gradually learn what our goals should be. The Vietnam War offers a tragic lesson on forcefully defining goals with little understanding of the problem and one's adversaries. The war was prosecuted under the leadership of Defense Secretary Robert McNamara. As both a Harvard MBA and a Harvard Business School professor, he exemplified the cool, rational application of planning and analysis to business. He confidently applied the same rigorous, systematic ways of thinking and managing to the war in Vietnam. Applying the mental model of MBO (management by objectives), it was war by numbers. How many enemy soldiers were killed in each campaign?

Knowing about his obsession with numbers, lower-ranked commanders would fudge the figures to please the top brass. The American public refused to be fooled. While the body count of enemy soldiers showed the US to be winning by a margin of 1 to 10, live reporting by intrepid correspondents in the field told a story of carnage and inhumane acts. Ultimately, the US had to withdraw ignominiously despite their overwhelmingly superior technology and military arsenal. McNamara misjudged the Vietnamese's will and determination to rid themselves of foreign domination. Towards the end of his life, he admitted, "We were wrong, terribly wrong."

*"The American soldiers were brave, but courage is not
enough. David did not kill Goliath just because he was
brave. He looked up at Goliath and realized that if he
fought Goliath's way with a sword, Goliath would kill
him. But if he picked up a rock and put it in his sling, he
could hit Goliath in the head and knock Goliath down and
kill him. David used his mind when he fought Goliath. So
did we Vietnamese when we had to fight the Americans."*
General Vo Nguyen Giap

4. There is more than one possible answer to a problem. During
the Second World War, when Japanese forces were sweeping through
Asia, Churchill declared that Singapore would never fall as it was an
impregnable fortress. The city was protected by huge gun placements
pointing south to the sea. To the north of the island on the Malayan
mainland hundreds of miles of treacherous jungle, mangroves and
swamps appeared to be impenetrable. But the Japanese forces had other
ideas. They defied conventional logic and came from the north unexpect-
edly and overwhelmed the British.

How to apply the indirect approach

The indirect approach is best whenever complex systems evolve in an
uncertain environment, and whenever the effects of our actions depend
on the ways in which others respond to them. How may we develop
greater facility in applying this in our work?

- **Adopt an alternative to our customary way of thinking:**
  We are trained to be action-biased, so there is a tendency to
  quickly identify the solutions. This will lead us to taking the direct
  approach. Pause and ask instead, "How can I think about this
  differently?" In the three cases that we have discussed, how
  would you assess the challenges and options before you?

- **Examine and critique your objectives:** McNamara's marching orders from President Johnson were to use their massive firepower to bring the Vietnamese to their knees. He did not examine and critique this objective. He later admitted that he did not understand the perspectives of his Vietnamese adversaries. They didn't fight because they were anti-American. All they wanted was self-determination. In contrast, Sirolli reinterpreted the objectives of their mission. It was to help to lift the African people out of poverty – not necessarily to teach them to grow food.

- **Start with small steps:** Choose something relevant to the task. One thing will lead to another. There will be waiting time as you iterate and experiment. But it is through doing that new information, of many kinds, becomes available.

- **Use a variety of mental models:** There is no single model for every situation. We need to build it and test it out. Every case is different. What if Bill Gates had allowed for the possibility that not all communication devices had to use Windows as the OS? Would today's narrative on smartphones and e-readers have taken a decidedly different trajectory?

- **Think like a generalist:** It really doesn't help to behave like an expert and impose one's views on others. This mindset is passe. Instead, adopt a curious and open mindset. Everything is contextual. Be a fox rather than a hedgehog.

> *"The fox knows many things.*
> *The hedgehog knows one big thing."*
> Archilochus, Greek poet

24

PERSPECTIVE- TAKING

Integrating different perspectives
is a key leadership skill

"Many ideas grow better when transplanted into another mind than in the one where they sprang up."
Oliver Wendell Holmes,
American physician, polymath and poet

The parable of the six blind men encountering an elephant captures the essence of different perspectives. Each man is holding onto a different part of the elephant and reaches a conclusion about the animal on the basis of a single part of it. This is an allegory for the challenge that we all face in organizations. As the poet John Godfrey Saxe puts it, "each was partly in the right and all were in the wrong." In managing challenges in the complex environments that we face, we too may not possess a complete picture, but only a part of it. Seeking others' perspectives actively and humbly can enhance our effectiveness, and prevent fatal mistakes in decision-making. And for leaders, the burden is even greater. Unwillingness to seek different perspectives may lead to ill-advised decision-making that may inflict harm on the organization.

What is perspective-taking?
Perspective-taking is the ability to perceive a situation or understand a concept from another person's point of view and from how she is

reacting cognitively and emotionally to it. It is a powerful tool for resolving conflicts, designing products and services with the end-users in mind, creating a climate of creativity, bringing out a better version of ourselves, and becoming a better leader. All it takes is stepping outside ourselves and understanding someone else's worldview. But it's not as easy as it sounds.

Our brains are hardwired to protect us by placing us at the center of our world. It makes us the hero and relegates all others to supporting roles. Whenever we encounter any situation, we make sense of it by referencing our own experiences, beliefs and values as the baseline. And if we aren't self-aware, we find ourselves frustrated despite doing what we think is the best for people around us. By engaging in perspective-taking, we learn to move away from this egocentric mindset and reap the benefits of a broader, richer and more informed base of understanding of humanity. What we do will be in greater alignment with the constituencies that we wish to serve.

The benefits of perspective-taking

Those who regularly seek different perspectives will enjoy the following benefits:

1. Discover more than you thought you knew. If you are in a meeting with others to discuss and then decide on a course of action, by listening to the views expressed by others you'll avail yourself of more information than you possess. Some of the new information may confirm that you're on the right track. Or it may cause you to rethink what's on your mind because others closer to the situation have a different view. It also will help you become more aware of the implications of decisions that are to be made.

2. Keep your confirmation bias in check. Confirmation bias is the tendency to process information by looking for, or interpreting, information that is consistent with one's current beliefs. Though largely unintentional, it often results in ignoring information that contradicts one's beliefs. For example, you may be leaning toward recruiting one of three shortlisted candidates. When you listen to others who have interviewed the candidates, you're unconsciously looking for comments that will reinforce your belief that you're making the right choice. By being open to the inputs from others, you may realize that you've missed out on critical aspects during the interview process. Perhaps you had allowed yourself to be blindsided because this candidate came highly recommended by a good friend.

3. Help you discover creative options when negotiating. A well-known example occurred during the presidential campaign of Theodore Roosevelt in 1912. As Election Day approached, his campaign workers printed nearly three million pamphlets with a photograph of Roosevelt looking rugged and presidential. Then someone discovered that the photograph had a copyright. It would cost an enormously large sum to pay the copyright fee. What should they do? Pay up or tear up the pamphlets? Roosevelt's campaign manager chose neither of these options. He considered the perspective of the studio that owned the copyright. First, he knew they weren't aware that the pamphlets had been printed. Second, he recognized that the studio might benefit from the publicity generated. What he next did was a master stroke. This was the message he cabled: "We are planning to distribute millions of pamphlets with Roosevelt's picture on the cover. It will be great publicity for the studio whose photograph we use. How much will you pay us to use yours?" The studio promptly responded, "We have never done this before. But under the circumstances, we'd be pleased to offer you $250." The deal was done. Perspective-taking converted a potentially huge financial liability into a tidy profit.

> *"Know thy enemy; know thyself.*
> *A hundred battles; a hundred victories."*
> Sunzi

4. Become more end-user-centric. By seeking to understand the perspectives of the end-users, you practice customer-centricity. You become more empathetic of their frustrations, needs and expectations. What you then offer is focused on creating the experience that they desire. This is the secret to meeting the needs of the constituencies we serve. This has application in conflict resolution. By seeking to understand, you can come to a common ground faster. There's a bonus at the end of the process. The other parties feel listened to. Mutual trust is beginning. This works well in the sales process. Top-performing sales persons will place customers at the center of what they do.

5. Bring to light your own assumptions. If you have many years of experience and have achieved success in what you are doing, you will intuitively assess any challenge presented to you based on assumptions derived from past cases. This can turn out to be an experience or expertise trap. You may not question your assumptions anymore. We see this in doctors, engineers, detectives, scientists and business leaders. Although such cognitive biases are normal, they can lead to incorrect diagnoses or assessments. By intentionally seeking outside views from non-traditional sources, you can correct your assumptions before proceeding further. We'd do well to heed French poet Moliere's admonition, "The learned fool is more foolish than the ignorant one."

6. Invitation to challenge your thinking. In essence, you're looking for people capable of providing effective challenge. The higher up you are in the hierarchy, the more you will need this. People lower down are reluctant to speak truth to power. In the olden days of monarchy in Europe, kings would employ court jesters to entertain them and their retinue at the end of a royal feast. Their remit was to convey observations to the kings that none of his fawning courtiers dared to. It was a decidedly dicey gig, as one can imagine. For today's business heads, you probably will not find the equivalent of court jesters. By seeking different perspectives from diverse people, you will discover fallacies in your thinking.

7. Create an environment for innovation. A mix of people from different backgrounds with unique perspectives can help challenge organizational assumptions, uncover new ways of thinking, and prevent team members from getting afflicted by groupthink. Thought diversity can help organizations make better decisions because it triggers more creative information processing, which is often absent in homogeneous groups. To harness this power, organizations and leaders must consciously make choices to bring in people with different perspectives.

How to harness new perspectives

1. Be humble and seek to learn. You already have your perspective, which you likely won't change very much if you keep talking. At meetings, request others to offer their views before you share yours. Encourage contrarian views. Not only will you learn something and gain a new perspective, you will build your relationships with the other persons at the same time.

2. Be curious and ask, instead of telling. This applies to one-on-one conversations as a way to extend your listening and learning, and also applies to conversations in general. When you are curious about the world around you and ask questions to understand things, you are automatically expanding your perspective and horizons at the same time.

3. Spend time with new and diverse people. This could be people from different departments, new neighbors, or someone from another country, discipline or organization. The goal here is to get to know people with different experiences from you, so you can begin to see their perspectives.

4. Read more widely. Reading provides us new vistas and perspectives. Read new authors, new genres, new magazines, blogs and websites. If you only read materials related to your industry, or only read your favorite author, you are deepening your expertise which is already considerable. Get out of your comfort zone. Adopt the beginner's mindset by taking an interest in something completely new to you. If you decide to learn more about, say, wildlife conservation or film-making, you will find rich sources of ideas that you can bring back to your work and life. I recommend watching TED talks on a variety of topics. Movies and documentaries are great sources of ideas too.

5. Check how you are progressing. Make it a point to reflect regularly and examine how your perspectives and sensibilities have become more expansive and inclusive. What are three new perspectives you have acquired every month? How do they impact the way you think, lead and make decisions? Share your learning with others. This is a great way to create a learning culture.

25

HUMBLE LEADERSHIP

**Humble leadership raises individual
and organizational effectiveness**

*"A leader is best when people barely know he exists.
When his work is done, his aim fulfilled,
they will say: we did it ourselves."*
Laozi

The final chapter of this book is about a paradoxical idea: humble leadership. It is often misunderstood and flies in the face of conventional wisdom. Humility is unlikely to be the first quality that comes to mind when you think of leaders. We are all used to seeing leaders as outgoing, confident and charismatic. We habitually assume that without such personality traits, leaders can't be effective. Hence humble leadership is a contradiction in terms. Implicit in this dissonance is that humility and charisma are opposites. If the leader is humble, how is he going to rally and motivate people to achieve ambitious results?

This topic goes full circle back to the concept of leadership paradoxes that kicked off this book. When faced with ideas that appear to be diametrically opposite, such as charisma and humility, we may transcend our inner conflict by embracing them as interdependent and complementary as in *yin* and *yang* forces. By taking the both-and approach, we avail ourselves of the emergence of multiple truths. Experience and studies have shown that organizations with humble leaders can indeed achieve exceptional levels of success on a sustainable basis. But it is not just humility per se. Let's now unpack this rather curious leadership dynamic.

The tenuous link between charisma and leadership effectiveness

Conventional thinking has it that leaders need to be charismatic. There are two implicit assumptions behind this. Firstly, it presupposes that leadership is a function of personality. Some people will have more talent for leadership than others. This has been borne out conclusively in real-life settings. While leaders are both made and born, some gravitate to leadership roles more readily than others. Secondly, it is assumed that people with charisma will be better leaders than those who are not charismatic. This has been disproved again and again in historical and contemporary settings in business, politics and wartime situations.

Charisma is the quality of being able to attract, charm, and win the devotion of people around you. Leaders who possess charisma will have this edge over others who don't. But extreme charisma will lead to narcissism. People afflicted by this display arrogance and a sense of entitlement. Data on the performance of narcissistic leaders show that they ruin companies. Because they can be really magnetic and fascinating, they are able to seduce and sell their grandiose ideas to boards, investors and the workforce. They make commitments that they can't keep, ignore feedback and suggestions, and underestimate how difficult it is to implement their pet projects. Narcissistic leaders usually come with supersized egos that will soon alienate and polarize people who come in contact with them.

The story of high-flying Chinese entrepreneur Jia Yueting is an example. He once dreamed of challenging Netflix, Apple and Tesla all at once, announcing billions of dollars in deals to expand his company, LeEco, beyond video streaming and into smartphones, electric cars and sports media. His charm and charisma quickly attracted huge investments, and by 2015 his fortune was estimated at over $6B. It didn't take long for the facade to crack. With mounting debt accumulated under his rapid expansion plans, banks withheld credit lines, and lawsuits followed over missed payments. In 2019, Jia Yueting filed for bankruptcy in the US.

Jim Collins's study on leadership and organizational effectiveness

In 1996 Jim Collins began a 5-year pioneering study on high-performance organizations. He and his team set out to answer one question: Can a good company become a great company and if so, how? Out of the 1,435 Fortune 500 companies that Collins studied, only 11 cleared all the hurdles that he had set. They were able to garner stock returns at least three times the market for 15 years after a major transition period.

Collins found that these 11 companies had one thing in common: what he called "Level 5" leaders at the helm. These are executives that bring with them genuine personal humility blended with intense professional will. It was a downright heretical finding when this was first announced because in the US and the rest of the world almost everyone believed that CEOs should be charismatic and larger-than-life figures. Even today this still sounds incredible. If these 11 CEOs were put in a room with other people, it would be difficult to pick them out. They were quiet, self-effacing, reserved and even shy. But beneath the surface, each of them was fiercely ambitious, tremendously competitive, utterly tenacious and at the same time modest and humble.

What then is humble leadership?

> "Three precious things I hold fast and prize. The first is gentleness; the second frugality; the third is humility, which keeps me from putting myself before others."
> Laozi

> "Humility is the base and foundation of all virtues, and without it, no other virtues can exist."
> Miguel de Cervantes

In a 2014 study by Catalyst Research Center for Advancing Leadership Effectiveness of more than 1,500 employees from different demographics from Australia, China, Germany, India, Mexico and the US, it was found that when employees observed altruistic or selfless behaviors in their managers, they reported being more innovative, suggesting new product ideas and ways of doing work better. They were also more likely to engage in team citizenship behavior, going beyond the call of duty, picking up the slack for absent colleagues – all indirect effects of feeling more included. This was true for both men and women.

Humble leadership is a meta-competency that comprises five critical leadership factors:

1. **Service to others.** Such leaders view leadership as both a privilege and a responsibility. They lead with the purpose of serving others – the company, team, community and the world in a broader sense. While earning a livelihood is very important, people all come to work hoping to find a deep emotional connection with what they do. Only then will they bring their whole self to the work environment. They also are concerned about their career path and will not stay on in companies where their managers do not devote time to developing them or provide opportunities for them to achieve their potential.

2. **Awareness that they do not know everything.** Events are happening so fast that leaders run the risk of being starved of vital information. Knowledge, expertise and ideas are tucked away at different nodes in the organization network. Leaders who aren't plugged into the network will be shut out. It is only by being humble and building an open and trusting relationship with their people that they can tap into the rich store of ideas, opinions and counsel. This requires setting their ego aside, willing to be vulnerable and treating others with respect. They deeply value the different perspectives that others bring.

3. **Commitment to self-improvement.** They know that they are a work-in-progress and are always eager to listen to feedback. They are receptive to criticisms and are willing to admit their mistakes. By being open to ideas from all people, they role-model continuous learning and the spirit of curiosity and inquiry.

4. **Acting with courage and integrity.** They are aware that as leaders they are highly visible figures. What they say and do are consistent with the values that they espouse. In tough and morally ambiguous situations, they are willing to take personal risks for the greater good. And they do this consistently. Trust is a value that they hold to dearly. They trust their people and in turn people trust them.

5. **Holding people accountable for results.** They will create conditions for people's success, and they do not micro-manage. People all know that such leaders will hold them accountable for results. Rather than monitoring and tracking through performance matrixes, people are motivated by the bond that has been established with them. When success is attained, they generously give credit to the people.

The notion of humble narcissism

It is necessary to mention that humility in and of itself is meaningless. It must be accompanied by competence and confidence. This is consistent with our discussions in Chapter 18 regarding how leaders can win the trust and respect of others. Interpersonal warmth comes first but must be accompanied closely by competence.

Before we wrap up, it is useful now to discuss the concept of *humble narcissism*. While humility brings about many virtues and benefits, leaders need to adopt a nuanced approach in practicing it. Undoubtedly they will encounter numerous situations in which a certain measure of narcissism may make a difference between failure and success. There are four examples that come to mind:

1. If you are representing your firm in speaking to investors to seek funding, it would behoove you to act and sound confident. To a large extent, their judgment of your proposal is based on their impression of you. This may not be the time to hide your light under a bushel, if you will. But tempering your confidence must be your willingness to listen and being mindful of their questions and concerns.

2. Westerners are usually fairly confident in projecting themselves in discussions. East Asians tend to be more reserved and reticent. In business meetings, Asians inadvertently place themselves at a disadvantage because of their natural humility and modesty. Make no mistake about this. Asian leaders who do not confidently engage in the rather fast-paced and at times contentious tussle of ideas and opinions will be judged as unable to communicate and influence. This is the key reason for disqualifying Asians from higher positions even though they are able to deliver outstanding business results. Culturally Asians prefer not to seek attention. They think their work will speak for itself. Such a misguided mindset will relegate them to the sidelines in the corporate world. My suggestion is for them to get out of their comfort zone, be bold and dial up their presence by a couple of notches. Only then can they claim their rightful seats at the table.

3. Women leaders across all cultures are generally kind, patient and empathetic. This makes them great leaders as humility is a natural trait. However, in the business space dominated by hard-charging and self-promoting male executives, too much humility will work to their disadvantage. Women leaders, like Asian leaders in general, can position themselves for greater

influence and success by blending humility with an appropriate level of narcissism.

4. There will be times when leaders will have to make a judgment call after seeking inputs. Differing ideas are great. Soon it's time to decide, although many stakeholders remain divided on the best course of action. Humble leaders must now rise to the occasion and point the way forward. That's what they are paid to do. This is when appropriate narcissism will inspire confidence in people.

INDEX

ABOUT THE
AUTHOR

BH TAN is a leadership consultant, executive coach and author specializing in
leadership development in a culturally
diverse environment. He is the president
of Lead Associates based in Singapore.
He has coached CEOs, presidents, VPs,
senior managers and executive leadership teams in APAC, the United States
and Europe.

He is particularly interested in the
development of women leaders, Mil-
lennials and Gen Z. These are the three constituencies that will reshape
leadership in the Digital Age. The workforce of the future deserves a
more collaborative, human-centric and empowering playing field. This
shift will happen only if all organizations commit to gender equality in
their leadership ranks, especially at the highest levels.

BH is a lifelong student of Eastern and Western thinking and leadership. He takes a wide interest in current affairs and delights in being the
devil's advocate in conversations. Married with two grown-up daughters,
he is the author of three books on leadership: *The First-Time Manager in
Asia*, *Leading with New Eyes* and *The Way of the Leader*.

For more information, you may contact him at bh@leadassociates.
com.sg. Visit his website at www.leadassociates.com.sg